629.2275   HOLLIDAY
           MOTORCYCLE
PANORAMA
                    795

616160 ✓

629.2275   HOLLIDAY
           MOTORCYCLE
PANORAMA

616160 ✓

Santa Clara County Free Library

California

Alum Rock	Milpitas	{ Calaveras / Community Center / Sunnyhills
Campbell		
Cupertino	Morgan Hill	
Gilroy	Saratoga	{ Quito / Village
Los Altos { Main / Woodland	Stanford-Escondido	

Research Center-Cupertino

For Bookmobile Service, request schedule

MOTORCYCLE PANORAMA

MOTORCYCLE

BOB HOLLIDAY

ARCO PUBLISHING COMPANY, INC.
New York

PANORAMA

A Pictorial Review of Design and Development

By the same author

NORTON STORY

Published 1975 by Arco Publishing Company, Inc.
219 Park Avenue South, New York, N.Y. 10003

Copyright © 1974 by Bob Holliday

Library of Congress Catalog Card Number 74-14052

ISBN 0-668-03647-8

Printed in Great Britain

CONTENTS

Continued overleaf

A Note to the American Edition

All prices included in the text have been given in British pounds sterling and no attempt has been made to translate them into dollars. At the time of this writing (late 1974), both the dollar and the pound were floating in the international money market and the value of one in terms of the other was changing from day to day. Also, the author took his prices from the only market he was sure of—that is, the British, where the imported models had found their final price after dealer markups, import duties, costs of transportation, etc. And as any motorcyclist knows, there is a great deal of bargaining between buyer and seller, even when the seller is an established dealer. All of this conspires to make any translation of price from pounds to dollars confusing and perhaps misleading. We have retained the British prices only as a means of comparing the costs of particular models.

INTRODUCTION

SINCE the 1890s, when the first petrol propelled two-wheelers were marketed commercially, nearly 2,000 different makes of motorcycle have been offered to the public. Many of their begetters were 'two-men-and-a-boy' concerns, producing perhaps only a small batch of a single type and then fading away within a year or so leaving little else on the pages of history than a name, and sometimes not even an address.

But in the main, the world's motorcycle makers can, or could, look back on long periods of years, producing wide ranges of machines constantly up-dated from season to season. It has not been unusual for one firm to catalogue as many as twenty different basic models, and to permute that number by optional specification variations.

Over thirty nations have had their motorcycle constructors, and well over half still have them. A computer could doubtless calculate how many individual sorts and kinds of machines have been made, but what a memory it would need to be given! And this is a book that, with but a hundred examples, spans a near-century during which the motorcycle has been developing. As an all-embracing review of design progress, it is totally inadequate, but that was never its purpose. It really stemmed from a question asked by a librarian acquaintance. 'There's an increasing interest in motorbike books,' he said. 'Is there one that shows the main changes that have been made, from the year dot to the present day—mostly with pictures?'

At first it seemed simple. All one had to do was collect a suitable number of illustrations and write something about each of them. But what was a 'suitable' number? A list of all the machines I first thought should be included proved much too long and repetitive and it was doubtful if pictures of some of the models were still in existence, or if sufficient factual information was still available to provide the captions.

So, with the advice of friends, the present 'ton-up' final selection was eventually made. Of course, it should have included the 1917 belt-cum-chain New Fangle. And—what, no mention of a speedway Backslider? And, fancy leaving out the three-stroke Moto-Moer! Perhaps next time. . . .

For the present, here are one hundred representatives of the motorcycle makers' craft, culled from around the world, east to Japan and west into the United States of America. They are widely assorted in age, size, type and usage. They are all quite different. Some are, or were, highly successful best-sellers; some were never sold at all. Apart from being two- or three-wheelers, what they aggregate in common is a wealth of diverse ingenuity, and the examples have been chosen principally to pinpoint some of the most significant, trendsetting, unusual and, perhaps, even unique features of design and construction that have shown up as time rolled by.

The propulsion of a 'motorcycle' by means of a petrol-burning internal combustion engine was first achieved by the German, Gottlieb Daimler—almost accidentally. Daimler, who had earlier worked with Dr A. N. Otto, patentee of the four-stroke engine principle, was experimenting with petrol motors for marine use, and in 1885 he fitted one of these engines into the wooden framework of a 'boneshaker' bicycle. It worked, but it was not truly a motor

Credit for America's first mechanically-propelled two-wheeler is given to L. D. Copeland, of Philadelphia, who, in 1884, converted a US-built Star racing bicycle to steam propulsion. Contrary to 'penny-farthing' practice, the smaller wheel was at the front

servatism of a horse-loving nation. Even after the four miles an hour speed limit had been raised, in 1896, to fourteen miles an hour, English motorcycle progress was slow and virtually confined to tricars and quadricycles.

On the Continent the motorcycle, as a single-track vehicle, began to catch on as a useful means of transport when the Werner brothers went into commercial production with their 'motocyclette', which was based on a safety-bicycle frame having a small petrol engine mounted over, and driving, the front wheel. The idea was widely copied on both sides of the Channel and in the USA, and by 1900 motorcycling was established in Britain.

With characteristic quick reaction to a new idea, the Americans took to motorcycling enthusiastically. Between 1900 and 1905 a score of manufacturers set up in business and several were already exporting machines to England, notably Harley-Davidson (now the sole survivor), Indian, Mitchell, Orient, Pierce-Arrow, Reading Standard and Royal. It was with an American Mitchell engine that the Stevens brothers, of Wolverhampton, powered their first motorcycle, the forerunner of the famous AJS marque.

The first five years of the twentieth century were a period of experiment. While the motorised-cycle type of machine persisted, its top-heaviness and proneness to sideslip on the muddy, slimy road surfaces of the day brought about many attempts to evolve a more stable lay-out. Every possible engine-mounting position was tried, even to a location within the rear wheel.

So many makers in both Europe and the USA dabbled with so many varieties of construction that the infant motorcycle industry almost choked itself with over-

bicycle for it had a pair of small outrigged supplementary wheels. However, the engine, which included internal flywheels and a mechanically-operated exhaust valve, opened the way to the rapid and enormous growth of the automotive industry.

It was in Germany and France that the petrol motor soon began to show its superiority over the steam and electric prime movers that were its rivals as the nineteenth century neared its close. In Britain, inventors and experimenters, such as Edward Butler (who was actually prohibited from driving his Petrol-Cycle on open roads) were hampered by restrictive legislation and the con-

production. Early enthusiasm for the new means of transport dwindled as the customers realised that they were acting as guinea-pigs for manufacturers who seemed unable to agree on what a motorcycle should be, or how to develop it into a safe and reliable vehicle. In Britain, in 1904, when the law first required number plates to be carried, some 22,000 machines were registered. The following year saw the addition of a further 12,000, but thereafter the sales graphs dropped alarmingly.

Two factors were largely instrumental in stopping the rot. One was the near-universal adoption by the industry of the method of mounting the engine in a position corresponding to that of the crank bracket on a pedal cycle. By locating the heaviest part of the machine—the crankcase, with its flywheels and crank assembly—below the hub line, the low centre of gravity so essential for

Parisian pioneers of cranked pedal action for bicycles, Pierre Michaux and his son Ernest constructed the first known powered single-tracker in 1869 when they fitted a small Perreaux steam engine to one of their 'boneshakers'

the good handling of a single-tracker was at last achieved. The arrangement was destined to continue, with very few exceptions, as common practice to this day.

The other major influence on the pioneer motorcycle movement was the commencement, in 1907, of the Isle of Man Tourist Trophy race series. In Europe and the United States, where there were no restricting speed limits, engineers had, almost from the start of motoring, benefited from experience gained through submitting their machinery to the testing conditions imposed by races. On the British mainland, racing on public roads was, and of course still is, completely prohibited. This rule, together

9

with the stringently-enforced maximum speed limits, undoubtedly accounted largely for the early superiority in performance and swift advances in design of foreign motorcars and motorcycles.

In 1904, the Automobile Club of Great Britain and Ireland, later the Royal Automobile Club, had taken advantage of the Isle of Man government's ability to allow racing on its roads and had used a round-the-island course for eliminating trials to select a team for that year's Gordon Bennett race in Germany. A year later, the Auto Cycle Club, as the Auto Cycle Union was then called, made use of the car racers' Island Tourist Trophy organisation to pick a team of motorcyclists to represent Britain in the continental International Cup event. When this fixture fizzled out in 1906, the ACC decided to hold its own Tourist Trophy Race and, on 28 May 1907, the plan was duly carried out.

It is impossible to guess what motorcycles would be like, or what would have become of the movement, had there never been a TT. It soon became the criterion by which everything was judged; it provided a proving ground for every aspect of technical design; and under its spell the development of the motorcycle, especially the British motorcycle, surged ahead, far outstripping that of the motorcar.

For some seven years, until the First World War, the motorcycle industry in Britain enjoyed a state of stable prosperity. Companies like Triumph, Matchless, AJS, Sunbeam and Rudge-Whitworth consolidated reputations for making sound machines in large quantities. There was no longer any need for reliance on foreign designs, and proprietary engine builders, such as JAP, supplied the power for many notable constructors. Indeed, it was a time when pride in craftsmanship was at a peak and, from the smallest to the largest, the factories' design and production men vied with one another to achieve optimum performance from the best available engineering techniques.

After World War I came the worldwide expansion of personal transport. Morris, Austin and Ford brought the motorcar to the ordinary citizen and even though good new cars could be bought for around £100, the popularity of the two-wheelers grew apace. Bicycles were turned out by the million and the ranks of motorcycle makers grew to such an extent that there was not room for all of them to exhibit at the annual show held at Olympia, in London. Scooters, sidecars and three-wheelers swelled the throng. By 1924, more than 500,000 motorcycles were registered in the UK and in 1929 the total was close on three-quarters of a million. The variety of types and diversity of design seemed boundless. Small wonder that so many of the examples in this book cover only that decade in the eighty-eight years' history of motorcycles—over one-third of the hundred models featured in this book.

The first few hectic years that followed World War I saw many of the smaller marques, founded on enthusiasm and gratuities, disappear, but the major firms kept pace with the apparently unending demand. The two great Birmingham producers, BSA and Ariel, were able to build over 1,000 a week by 1928 and there were weeks in 1929 when the BSA plant reached the 2,000 mark.

Then came the Wall Street crash and the depression of the 1930s. One after another, the factories got into financial difficulties. Many closed down. Some kept going by amalgamations and mergers. Others sought to stay alive by diversification into other industries. It was a bad patch for the

innovators. Many a promising project had to be shelved until better days returned, or else had only a brief life because the firm was too short of money to give it a proper launching.

Strangely, as the registration figures plummetted the sporting side of motorcycling flourished. The clubs held together and many new ones were formed. Races at Brooklands and Donington drew big entries and reliability trials developed into cutthroat contests. The technicians went back to their drawing boards to devise such celebrated sports mounts as the Ariel 'Red Hunters', the BSA 'Stars', the 'International' Nortons and the Triumph 'Tigers' and 'Speed Twins'.

The United States, which could claim to have had over eighty different manufacturers, had long since lost interest in motorcycles, to the point where only the pioneer Indian and Harley-Davidson companies were left in business. But on the European continent, always motorcycle-minded, a big change was taking place. With the encouragement of their prestige-

When James L. Norton built his first Norton motorcycles he used French-made Clement engines similar to the unit that powered this 1902 Clement-Garrard lightweight

seeking dictators, Italian and German constructors were threatening the long-held 'British supremacy' in the speed sphere. As the 1930s ended, the writing was clearly on the wall. An Italian, riding an Italian machine, held the World's motorcycle speed record and a German, on a German machine, had won the Senior TT Race. Both machines were multi-cylindered, and it seemed that the days of Britain's all-conquering 'single-lungers' were ending when World War II began.

It is on record, however, that despite having to adapt to low-octane petrol, British singles were Senior and Junior TT winners after the war up to 1955, which was the year when, for the first time since 1907, all the Trophies—and all but three of the places—were taken by either Italian or German machines.

On the roadster side of the business, the traditional British 'thumper' was finding the going tough. Post-war Italy set a world-wide fashion for scooters, the two main producers, Lambretta and Vespa, swamping the markets with increasingly sophisticated models. Germany and France led the field with another type of 'peoples' transport', the pedal-equipped 50cc moped, vast quantities of which were built by NSU, VeloSolex and Mobylette, to name but three of the scores of marques available.

Nearly all these runabouts were two-stroke powered and they sparked off the tremendous advances that have been made in a type of engine which, before World War II, was regarded as a cheap-to-make but relatively inefficient unit, fit only for what were derisively called 'pip-squeak' mounts. Modern racing two-strokes produce outputs in the 70bhp bracket and one of them has lapped the TT circuit at 105·5mph.

Although Britain had flirted with scooters in the 1920s and had pioneered mopeds in the 1930s, when they were known as autocycles, the English factories missed out on the scooter boom and never really got a footing in the pedal market. Instead, Britain's backroom boys mostly held their faith in 'big bangers', with particular attention to the parallel-twin formation so notably promoted by Edward Turner's famous Speed Twin in 1937. The potentialities of this form of engine were dramatically demonstrated when a Norton Domi-racer became the first push-rod engined machine to achieve a 100mph TT lap.

Such concentration on large-capacity machines gave the continental constructors a golden opportunity in the under-250cc markets. In addition to mopeds and scooters, they developed a wide range of very well-made lightweights of advanced and varied design. Such marques as NSU, DKW, Kreidler, Guzzi, MV, Mondial, Ducati,

Morini and Montesa shared the honours in the below-quarter-litre classes of international races. Britain's fortunes in the grands prix, for so long based on the larger capacity classes, reached rock bottom in 1957 when, for the first time at a TT, not one of the first three places in any of the five races was taken by a British machine.

Italian dominance of the lightweight field took a setback in 1961 when an altogether new marque appeared among the lists of TT winners. Japanese Hondas gained hat-tricks in the 125 and 250cc events. The infiltration from the Orient had begun in 1959 when a party of Honda personnel and riders arrived in the Isle of Man with a shipment of 125cc ohc twin machines that surprised westerners, who until then had little idea of the progress the Japanese had made. Only one of the five little machines failed to finish and, at their first crack at a TT, Honda won a manufacturers team prize.

Although it was the Honda company which initiated the Oriental invasion of the motorcycle strongholds of the West, they were soon challenged by the two-strokes of their compatriots Suzuki and Yamaha. The competition, both on the tracks and in the markets, was furious. Incredibly potent and intricate machines were devised and there seemed to be no limit to ingenuity or expense. When 50cc racing was popular, Suzuki produced a *three*-cylinder engine of that capacity. Yamaha had a water-cooled two-stroke 'four' for the quarter-litre class and Honda's 297cc 'six', so successful in the later 1960s, remains one of the miracles among motorcycles. What realms of complexity this rivalry would have developed can only be guessed at, for the formulation of rules limiting under-250cc machines to two cylinders and six speeds halted Japanese factory participation in international road races.

It did not, however, diminish their designers' inventiveness, as witness the recently revealed Yamaha Omniphase answer to engine vibration problems that engineers have always believed to be economically insurmountable. Development of this oh-so-simple method of sharing an engine's flywheel mass between the crankshaft and a contra-rotating, chain-driven balance shaft will be watched with the utmost interest by technicians everywhere.

While Japan was making inroads into the established capacity classes, manufacturers in the West were working on the demands— stemming from the United States—for bigger mounts, soon to be known as 'Superbikes.' In general, these have grown from the pre-war 500cc parallel-twin types, increasing in stages through 650, 700, and 750cc to 800cc and over. As the weights of their reciprocating components have required equivalent compensation on a 360° crankshaft, their out-of-balance mid-stroke forces have multiplied accordingly, not only bringing about greater vibration tendencies but also imposing the need for heavier bearings with more robust supports.

To help insulate the rider from engine vibration, Nortons evolved their Isolastic rubber-mounting arrangements for the 750cc Commando models. To achieve smoothness, as well as a compact engine form, other makers followed the lead, set in 1965 by MV, and turned to the 120° throw three-cylinder unit which provides perfect balance. The 750cc BSA/ Triumph units are good examples and the 980cc dohc Laverda 1000 is the biggest 'three' so far. Particularly interesting is its unusual crankshaft arrangement in one plane—when the two outer pistons are at top dead centre the middle one is at the bottom of its stroke.

And so, as the powered single-tracker nears its centenary, what next? The Wankel engine, with its so-called rotary-piston layout, is now a practical proposition, already in motorcycle production. Or will the sheikhs who control the Arabian oil wells send us back to steam, or forward to electricity?

Whatever comes, let us touch our crash hats to the memory of Gottlieb Daimler, the first man ever to tweak a twist-grip.

London, 1974   BOB HOLLIDAY

HISTORIANS generally agree that the world's first workable petroleum-engined motor bicycle was built by Germany's celebrated inventor-engineer, Gottlieb Daimler (1834-1900). His vertical, single-cylinder power unit of 1885, developed from an earlier horizontal pattern, was capable of 700-800rpm, had internal flywheels, a mechanically (cam) operated exhaust valve and an automatic (suction) inlet valve admitting the petrol/air mixture from a surface carburettor; ignition was by the hot-tube method. The first design of Daimler motorcycle (patented in 1885) featured belt drive from engine shaft to rear wheel and a type of twist-grip handlebar control. An improved version, first ridden in 1886, had belt-drive to a countershaft on which a pinion engaged with an internally toothed ring on the rear wheel. This machine was destroyed by fire and the picture here reproduced is of a replica which is now preserved in a Munich museum.

BUTLER PETROL-CYCLE, 1887 Great Britain

AN Englishman, Edward Butler, born in 1863, was the first experimenter who set out to produce a marketable vehicle combining cycle features with petrol propulsion. His original Petrol-Cycle design of tricycle, patented in 1884, specified a two-stroke engine operating on the Clerk-cycle system. This produced insufficient power and Butler designed his own four-stroke (Otto cycle) unit with horizontal cylinders, one on each side of the rear wheel which incorporated 6:1 epicyclic gearing that allowed a working 600rpm. Battery and coil ignition replaced his earlier electrostatic ('Wimshurst machine') arrangement. A spray-jet carburettor with a float chamber would have made this clever inventor a very wealthy man if his patents had been maintained. As it was, the 4mph Locomotives Act, and a lack of financial backing, killed the Petrol-Cycle within two years of its introduction, the prototype being broken up to recover the value of the brass and copper used in its construction. Edward Butler lived until 1940, researching and writing on engineering matters.

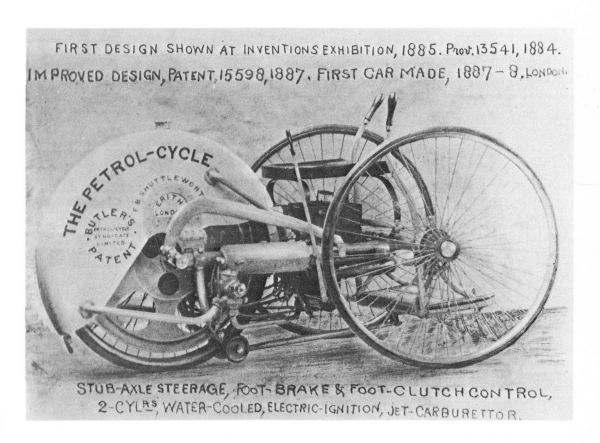

FIRST DESIGN SHOWN AT INVENTIONS EXHIBITION, 1885. Prov. 13541, 1884. IMPROVED DESIGN, PATENT, 15598, 1887. FIRST CAR MADE, 1887-8, LONDON.

THE PETROL-CYCLE

BUTLER'S F B SHUTTLEWORTH ERITH LOND. PETROL-CYCLE SYNDICATE LIMITED PATENT

STUB-AXLE STEERAGE, FOOT-BRAKE & FOOT-CLUTCH CONTROL, 2-CYLRS WATER-COOLED, ELECTRIC-IGNITION, JET-CARBURETTOR.

HILDEBRAND & WOLFMULLER, 1894   Germany

THE distinction of being the world's first motorcycle manufacturers on a commercial scale rests with a group of Munich engineers —the brothers Heinrich and Wilhelm Hildebrand, Alois Wolfmuller and Hans Greisenhof. Their attempts, begun in 1892, to power bicycles, first with steam and then with petrol engines, had proved unsuccessful but in 1894 they completely abandoned the cycle frame and evolved a specially designed machine of open-frame type within which was mounted a twin-cylinder four-stroke engine with connecting rods driving overhung cranks on the rear axle, after the manner of the Butler Petrol-Cycle. Absence of any flywheel effect was in part overcome by rubber straps to assist the idle compression stroke. The straps are missing in the accompanying picture but the attachments on con-rod and frame can be seen. Water for cooling the 90mm × 117mm cylinders was carried in the curved tank-cum-rear mudguard. Weighing 115lb, the machine could attain a speed of 24mph. Included in the patents was the word 'motorrad' (motorcycle). At one time, 1,200 people were employed at the Munich works but, inexplicably, production ceased just when petrol-driven bicycles and tricycles were becoming popular.

HOLDEN, 1897   Great Britain

PATENTED in 1894, and expressly intended for commercial production, was the Holden motorcycle, brainchild of a distinguished engineer, Col H. Capel Holden. As with the Butler and the Hildebrand & Wolfmuller machines, the horizontally-disposed four-stroke engine drove the rear wheel directly by connecting rods and cranks, but this was the first four-cylinder motorcycle ever made. Many ingenious and original ideas were incorporated in the design. The inlet valves were automatic but the exhaust valves were rocker-operated by a longitudinal camshaft driven by worm gear and chain from the rear axle. Pedals drove the front wheel through internal gearing. Coil ignition (with a camshaft-driven distributor) and a surface carburettor were other features. The aircooled model of 1897 pictured here weighed 123lb and had a maximum speed of about 25mph. A more powerful (420rpm) water-jacketed version sold widely between 1899 and 1902, when production ceased.

DE DION-BOUTON, 1899 France

FRENCHMEN Count Albert de Dion, industrialist, and Georges Bouton, engineer, went into partnership in 1883 to manufacture and market road vehicles, originally with steam engines. In 1895 they produced a 50mm × 70mm $\frac{1}{2}$hp single-cylinder four-stroke petrol engine based on Gottlieb Daimler's design. It weighed 40lb and ran up to 1,800rpm. So successful was this prototype that, in a variety of ratings reaching as high as 8hp, it was developed to drive many makes of machine in many countries, being built under licence in England as the MMC by the Motor Manufacturing Co of Coventry.

De Dions' application of their own engines was chiefly to tricycles, with the power unit mounted behind, and directly geared to, the differential rear axle. The illustration here is taken from the company's catalogue of 1899, when the factory at Puteaux à Seine covered an area of over 30,000 square yards. In that year a $2\frac{3}{4}$hp model averaged 28mph in the Paris-Bordeaux-Paris race. Surface carburation was used and a strong selling point was electric ignition employing easily replaceable dry batteries (capable of 300 working hours). Speed was regulated by advancing and retarding the spark.

DE DION-BOUTON, 1899 France

'THIS bicycle has been made with a view to satisfying our customers who always prefer riding this style of machine, but, of course, it does not possess the advantages of our tricycle in many technical and practical ways.' That was how the contemporary motoring writer, H. O. Duncan, translated the 1899 De Dion-Bouton catalogue's description of this $1\frac{1}{2}$hp motorcycle. The belt

drive to the rear-wheel gearing could be slackened or tightened to give a free-engine and simple, variable-speed effect, by means of a patented 'rubber expanding pulley.' The fixed pedals acted as footrests only. Machines were built to customers' special orders and never achieved anything like the popularity of the tricycle types.

WERNER, 1899   France

RUSSIAN-born brothers Eugene and Michel Werner, who had settled in Paris, began experiments with petrol-engined bicycles in 1896-7. In 1899 they had standardised, and were selling in large numbers, the type of 'motocyclette' pictured here. Of 217cc (62mm × 72mm), the Hippolyte Labitte-designed engine had an automatic inlet valve over a cam-operated side exhaust valve, and an interesting feature was the method by which the mixture from the surface carburettor tank was fed through the steering column. A handlebar twist-grip controlled the speed by advancing and retarding the spark, which was battery and coil produced, as with the De Dion system. This machine was constructed as a complete entity and was not just a pedal-cycle with a 'clip-on' engine. Although smooth-running and relatively reliable, these mounts became known as 'demons for sideslip.'

In 1901, the Werners introduced an entirely new model which successfully solved the 'where to put the engine' problem and set a fashion that was to endure for over seventy years. De Dion engines were mounted vertically between the bases of the front down-tube and the seat pillar, the pedal gear bottom-bracket being moved aft of the crankcase, whose mass now helped to achieve the low centre of gravity needed to give the machine optimum stability.

ROYAL ENFIELD, 1902   **Great Britain**

THE success of the Werner 'motocyclette' led to many copies, one of which was this Royal Enfield machine of 1902. The 211cc Belgian-built Minerva engine had its crankcase split horizontally. To achieve a slip-free drive, the belt was crossed and applied to the rear wheel. Among several other refinements were front and rear band brakes, the latter being operated by the Eadie back-pedalling arrangement. The price of this machine was £50 and it was the first motorcycle produced by the Enfield Cycle Co which, from 1900, had made De Dion-engined tricycles.

CLAIMING, over a long period of years, to be one of the oldest motorcycle factories in the world, the Excelsior Motor Co Ltd originated as Bayliss, Thomas & Co Ltd in 1881, making bicycles. The first powered machines appeared in 1896, fitted with De Dion engines built under licence in the Excelsior works. Later, MMC engines were used and the 1902 machine here pictured has one of these units. The method of mounting the engine forward of the front down-tube was popular at this period, but many makers found it necessary to guard against frame breakage by various strengthening devices. The arrangement of bracing members at the steering head, as seen here, was typical of the times.

PHELON-RAYNER, 1902

Great Britain

AN extremely practical answer to the problem of where to mount the engine came from Yorkshire in 1900, when Joah Phelon and Harry Rayner, who were later joined by Richard Moore, began building motorcycles at Cleckheaton. As this photograph of a 1902 Phelon-Rayner shows, their method was to use the power unit itself as a main part of the frame, while four long rods, from steering head to bottom bracket, served the dual purpose of securing cylinder to crankcase and substituting for the normal front down-tube. The idea was reproduced under licence by the Humber company and was perpetuated throughout the long life of the P & M (Phelon & Moore) motorcycle ranges which succeeded the type illustrated.

NOT only was the Orient motorcycle a pioneer American machine, first appearing in 1900, but it was also among the earliest US-built mounts to be exported to Britain, examples having crossed the Atlantic soon after production was started by the Waltham Manufacturing Co, of Waltham, Massachusetts. In 1902 Orient machines 'from 2¼ to 3¾hp actual' were being advertised, as in the accompanying picture, by the Remington Automobile & Motor Agency, of Tothill Street, Westminster, London.

The model depicted is fitted with a French-built Aster proprietary engine having a horizontally-split bronze crankcase and an automatic inlet over a mechanically-operated exhaust valve arrangement, with the exhaust port at the rear of the cylinder. An unusual feature was the remotely situated spray carburettor, fed from a tank below the saddle. Transmission was by direct belt and the long-wheelbase 'frame construction has been most carefully thought out, resulting in great rigidity, strength and minimum of vibration.' Battery and coil ignition was used and the only brake acted directly on the front tyre. No mudguards were fitted. It was claimed that in speed trials one of these machines 'did the mile in 1min 10·4sec—over 50 miles per hour—proving the Orient to be the fastest motor bicycle on the market.'

The only surviving Orient in Britain, restored by Mr N. Manby, of Oakham, Rutland, is still running. It has a different valve layout and a vertically split crankcase on which is cast the Orient name, suggesting that the Waltham company also made its own engines. Otherwise, this noble veteran is virtually identical with the model pictured.

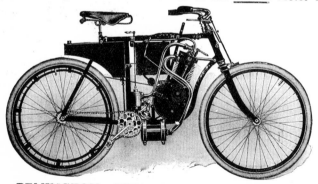

TRIUMPH, 1903   Great Britain

ONE of England's pioneer cycle firms—founded by two Germans, Siegfried Bettemann and Maurice Schulte—the Triumph company, of Coventry, began marketing 'clip-on'-type lightweight machines in 1901, using Belgian-built Minerva engines. In 1903, an all-British model was produced with an engine designed and made by John A. Prestwich, of Tottenham, London. Des-tined to become world-famous, JAP engines were the first British proprietary units and the Triumph version, based very much on the Minerva pattern, not only had a spray carburettor but also mechanical operation for both the side valves, the exhaust being placed forward to obtain the full benefit of air cooling.

JAMES, 1904   Great Britain

A MAJOR advance in motorcycle design was made in 1904 by the founder of the James Cycle Co Ltd, Harry James, who had been building high-grade bicycles since 1881 and Werner-motorised machines since 1901. His new departure took the form of a loop frame—one continuous length of tube in U-shape from steering head to saddle lug. A $3\frac{1}{2}$hp Belgian FN engine was mounted in a forward inclining position within the curve of the U. This formation, claimed to be the first loop frame ever made, was widely copied all over the world. A feature of this machine, rare in those days, was a separate float chamber for the carburettor.

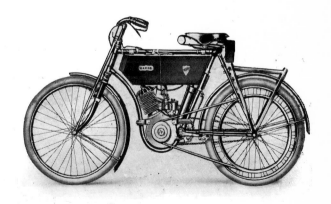

GEORGE M. HENDEE founded the Hendee Manufacturing Co Inc (later the Indian Co Inc) at Springfield, Mass, USA, in the days of the bicycle boom and in 1900, in association with mechanical engineer Oscar Hedstrom, he produced the first Indian motorcycle which had a rearward leaning, automatic inlet-over-side exhaust valve 1¾hp engine taking the place of the seat pillar. Commercial production began in 1902 and the type was continuously improved, a V-engined version being introduced in 1905. The single-cylinder 1905 model pictured here embodied a number of advanced features, such as all-chain drive with reduction gear from engineshaft to bottom bracket countershaft; an exceptionally neat form of front fork springing; and (first adopted in 1904) the unique Indian system of twist-grip control utilising rods and toggle joints. The carburettor is missing from the machine illustrated. Battery and coil ignition equipment was housed in the casing on the front down-tube. Oil was carried in the canister behind the cylinder, which was machined from solid steel.

FN, 1905   Belgium

IT WAS in 1901 that the Belgian ordnance factory, Fabrique Nationale d'Armes de Guerre, at Herstal, started making single-cylinder, belt-driven motorcycles and in 1904, at the Paris Salon, it entered the 'multi' market with a smooth-running, in-line, air-cooled four-cylinder mount of 363cc (45mm × 55mm). A Brown & Barlow carburettor fed the mixture through automatic inlet valves and a Bosch magneto was driven from the front end of the crankshaft. Spur gears took the drive, via a propellor shaft running through one of the frame members, to a crown wheel and pinion reduction gear. The whole transmission system was fully enclosed. The original rigid front fork was quickly changed to the neat leading-link arrangement shown. Growing over the years to 748cc, FN 'fours' were connoisseurs' machines and, though not built for racing, performed well in competitions. In 1923 the marque held the World's 1,000cc sidecar class 200-miles record at 66·39mph. Production of 'fours' ceased in the mid-1920s, by which time the engines had overhead inlet valves and side exhaust valves, operated from separate camshafts on each side of the block.

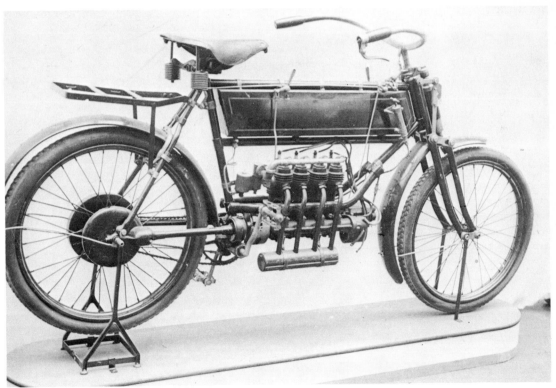

NSU—Neckarsulmer Fahrzeug-Werke—had, for some five years since 1901, been making in their Rhineland factory motorised cycles of the Minerva-engined 'clip-on' type when this much more substantial model was introduced. Although the crankcase carries an NSU engine-number plate, the company was using Z-L engines of around 200cc made by a French firm, Societé Francaise des Moteurs Zedel, in a works at Geneva, in Switzerland. The belt-tensioning jockey pulley, contracting-band rear brake, and neatly-stowed oilcan are noteworthy points.

MOTOSACOCHE, 1908   Switzerland

A SWISS firm, H. & A. Dufaux et Cie, estab- lished in 1891, like NSU (see previous picture) used Geneva-made Z-L engines for its lightweight machines, but patented in 1901 an ingenious method of power-unit mounting, intended originally as a conver- sion kit. The engine, tank and most of the ancillaries were assembled as an enclosed sub-unit that fitted into the diamond frame of a bicycle, being attached by clips and thumbscrews. Of the four-stroke type, the 211cc (62mm × 70mm) engine at first had accumulator and coil ignition, but this was replaced in 1907 by a high-tension magneto. Called the Motosacoche (literally 'motor- in-a-saddlebag'), it enjoyed a considerable vogue. The jockey pulley was cable-controlled to act as a 'clutch.' The Dufaux company, which also made MAG engines, adopted the Motosacoche name for all its motorcycle products over a long period of years.

LEA-FRANCIS, 1911   Great Britain

AFTER establishing a reputation for high-grade bicycle building, the Coventry firm of Lea & Francis turned to motorcycles in 1911 —and then not with lightweights but with a full-sized 650cc JAP V-twin engine, two-speed countershaft gearing and total enclosure for the final drive of the all-chain transmission. Dummy belt-rim brakes were fitted on both wheels; hitherto most manufacturers had got no further than cycle-type stirrup brakes for front wheels. Later, MAG engines were used by Lea-Francis and, until the firm turned from motorcycles to cars in 1926, these machines were renowned for their high standard of construction. In this picture the trade numberplate is attached to a removable section of the mudguard, designed to allow the quickly detachable wheel to be withdrawn.

ROYAL ENFIELD, 1912   Great Britain

AFTER producing its initial 1902 Werner-type motocyclette, the Enfield company at Redditch spent several years mainly making parts and fittings for the cycle and motor trades. In 1912, the firm came back into the complete-machine market with an advanced design of 2¾hp twin-cylinder lightweight— the Royal Enfield Model No 160. The designer was Osborne de Lissa and his 54mm × 75mm, 344cc, V-unit had horizontally-cast cylinder fins and side valves arranged transversely across the front and rear faces of the barrels. All-chain drive included a two-speed, free-engine gear based on a P & M method.

MOTOSACOCHE, 1912　　　　　　　　　**Switzerland**

THE similarity between this Motosacoche and the Model 160 Royal Enfield previously described is explained by the fact that O. de Lissa, who designed the 1912 Enfield, was in the same year engaged by the Dufaux brothers in Geneva and he produced a virtually identical model for them. Although the Enfield engines were made in Redditch and the Motosacoche units in Switzerland, both machines used the Enfield two-speed gear, but their ratios differed—5·75:1 and 8:1 in Geneva, and 6·25:1 and 8·25:1 in England. A year later de Lissa improved the Swiss engine to $3\frac{1}{2}$hp, with overhead exhaust valves. At the same time the $2\frac{3}{4}$hp RE was replaced by a 3hp model—the first motorcycle to have full dry-sump lubrication.

LEVIS, 1913　　　　　　　　　　**Great Britain**

A SMALL Birmingham firm, Hughes Butterfield Co (later Butterfields Ltd), had only been in the motorcycle business two years, building very light but well-made, reliable and speedy two-stroke machines, when it introduced a mount that, on its specification, should have been a great success. In the event (and that event may have been World War I), only one batch of the 1913 Levis Twin 348cc models ever left the Stechford works. This neat little machine, weighing just 110lb, had two 174cc (58mm

× 66mm) cylinders mounted side by side on a common, horizontally split, aluminium crankcase. The engine had only five moving parts—two pistons, two con-rods and one 180° crankshaft—and with a large outside flywheel it ran with car-like smoothness.

As with the Levis single-cylinder models, lubrication was by a constant-loss system that kept oil and petrol vapour apart. Standard models had chain-cum-belt $5\frac{1}{2}$:1 gearing, but a two-speed, free-engine Albion gear was an optional extra.

EXCELSIOR, 1913   U.S.A.

IGNEZ SCHWINN, founder of a firm that has made bicycles since they first appeared in the USA, set up the Excelsior Manufacturing & Supply Co in Chicago in 1908. This Excelsior Autocycle 1,000cc single-geared V-twin was built in 1913 and is seen as it was restored, after many years of rusting in a Cambridge, Mass, barn where

it was found in 1940 by former Indian Motorcycles executive Mr Ted Hodgdon (pictured). When the marque came to Britain it was known as the American X to distinguish it from the Birmingham-built Excelsiors. The leaf-spring front suspension is similar to that introduced in 1911 by Indians and used by them for many years.

THE first Veloce motorcycles, with the company's own four-stroke engines, were marketed in 1905 after a period, beginning in 1901, when Ormonde and Kelecom proprietary units had been fitted. The first two-stroke model emerged from the Spring Hill, Birmingham, factory at the end of 1912 for the 1913 season. To distinguish it from the heavier range, and to emphasise its light weight, it was called the Velocette—a trade name that was to appear on all the marque's tanksides thereafter.

The neat little newcomer had a single-port engine of 206cc (60mm × 73mm) fitted into a simple loop frame. The cast-iron cylinder and head were in one piece and an advanced feature was a patented automatic lubrication system, using exhaust gas pressure to draw oil from a separate crankcase compartment and deliver it to the main

and big-end bearings. Needle-valve adjustment controlled the supply. An over-hung crankpin and external flywheel were design features for many years in the firm's two-stroke models. Unbraced Druid front fork, stirrup front and belt-rim rear brakes, an AMAC or Senspray carburettor and a Bosch or UH magneto figured in the specification. Three versions were listed. The model illustrated, which was the prototype, had all-chain drive and a cable-operated two-speed gearbox. It cost 30 guineas; in open-frame, ladies' pattern, the price increased by two guineas. The third machine had direct belt drive, weighed 112lb and cost 25 guineas—a guinea in pre-decimalisation days, it may be recalled, being a rarely seen twenty-one shilling piece equivalent to-day to £1·05.

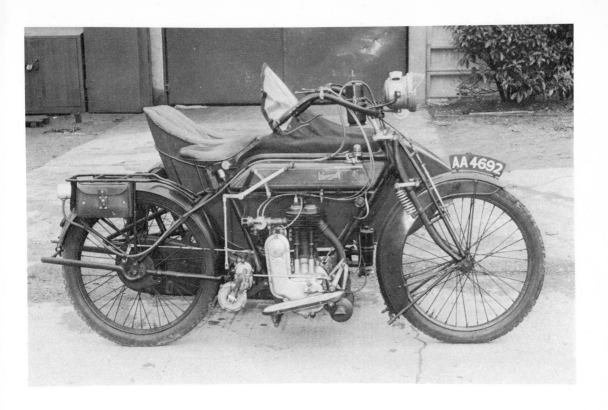

JAMES, 1914   Great Britain

FOLLOWING early experiments with unorthodox 'safety' models and proprietary
engines, the James Cycle Co produced, in
1911, a motorcycle hardheadedly aimed at
the commercial market and mostly made
in its own factory. Well ahead of most of
its contemporaries, it was claimed to be the
first motorcycle to incorporate all the
following selling points: all-chain drive with
two-speed gearbox; multi-plate clutch; kickstarter; transmission shock absorber; and
total enclosure for both chains, the primary
running in a cast aluminium oil bath.

Originally the gears were housed in a
malleable-iron casting integral with the
chain stays 'to provide strength, maintain
alignment and eliminate delicate adjustment.'
But neglect in lubricating the gears and
persistent ham-handed changing could cause
expensive trouble. A normal bolt-on type
two-, and later three-speed, box was designed
and fitted. The 1914 sidecar outfit here
illustrated has an additional refinement
in advance of its time—a full-sized drum
brake for the rear wheel.

ALTHOUGH its life-span of production lasted less than three years, the ABC, first marketed for 1920, has become a legend among motorcycles and the rare examples that have survived are some of the most valuable among collector's pieces. Soon after World War I had ended, that inventive genius, Granville Bradshaw, who had since 1913 been associated with the All British (Engineering) Co, designed for the Walton-on-Thames-based Sopwith Aviation Co, makers of the famous, but then no longer needed, Camel aeroplanes, a motorcycle that bristled with fresh ideas. His new ABC, costing from £110 upwards, had a 398cc (69mm × 54mm), ohv, air-cooled, transverse-twin engine built in unit with a four-speed gearbox operated by a car-type gate-change lever. Magneto ignition and a separate dynamo were other notable features. The unitised engine, flywheel, clutch and gearbox assembly was mounted in a duplex

cradle frame and leaf springing was used for both front and rear wheels. Final transmission was by chain, the original propellor-shaft design having proved unsatisfactory because of the large amount of movement afforded by the rear suspension. Drum brakes were used and much attention was paid to weather protection; in addition to deeply valanced mudguards there were legshields incorporated with the front frame members, and long footboards.

The ABC was fast—world records were broken with the prototype—and light; at 238lb a man of normal stature could easily lift it. Unfortunately, before there was time to eliminate the initial 'bugs'—the ohv gear was unreliable—the Sopwith company went into liquidation in 1921. A French concern, Société Francaise des Moteurs ABC (allied with Gnome et Rhône) continued production under licence until 1924.

ABC SKOOTAMOTA, 1919   **Great Britain**

ABOUT the same time as he was evolving the ABC transverse-twin motorcycle, Granville Bradshaw designed the ABC Skootamota, a very early example of the ultra-lightweight, mostly small-wheeled, runabouts that appeared on the market soon after World War I. These 'scooters', as they were called, enjoyed only a short-lived period of popularity and no one then dreamed that another world war would bring the type back into tremendous vogue.

The 1919 125cc Skootamota was originally produced for a marketing company, Gilbert Campling, of Albemarle Street, London. An open, unsprung frame of light gauge, duplicated tubing had the engine mounted on a bracket over the rear wheel, the single,

horizontal ohv cylinder pointing rearwards and balanced by a forward-facing, gear-driven magneto. Controls were extremely simple; a pedal protruding through the curved floorboard operated the rear contracting-band brake; on the handlebar were a throttle lever and inverted levers for the front brake (also contracting) and the exhaust-valve lifter. The external flywheel and driving sprocket were mounted on the camshaft, not on the mainshaft. Lubrication was by means of a hand-pump, feeding the oil from a compartment in the main tank supported above the engine. Without any forced-draught system, overheating was a problem with this otherwise advanced and neat-looking machine.

IT WAS way back in the first few years of this century that F. W. Barnes began to produce the machines that made such a name for themselves in motorcycling history. Initially, that name was Zenette, but it was soon changed to Zenith and when, in 1909, Freddie Barnes invented his celebrated Gradua gear, the marque gained such popularity with sporting riders that its success was almost an embarrassment. The ingenious method of providing variable gearing for the direct belt drive gave its users so great an advantage over their rivals that several organisers of the then highly popular hill-climb events refused to accept entries of Gradua Zeniths. Barnes turned this ban to publicity use, and 'Zenith Barred' became his trademark.

As with the Rudge Multi, an opening-closing engine pulley was used but, to maintain belt tension, the rear axle moved lengthwise in its fork. Control was by a tank-side winding handle, dubbed the 'coffee-grinder,' and there was an intricate arrangement of bevel gears, sprockets, cross-chain drive and compensating rods and levers. With early models, the belt-rim rear brake was cable-operated; later a lever system was devised, allowance having to be made for the longitudinal movement of the axle without altering the position of the pedal. An over-riding Bowden-controlled 'clutch' was also provided. The range of gearing afforded was from, approximately, 3:1 to 7:1. The 1920 model pictured has a 750cc side-valve JAP engine, but Barnes used practically every make of proprietary engine available. To wear a Sidcot suit and a flying helmet, and to have a flapper on the bracket of one's own Zenith Gradua, was the great ambition of many a young dog fifty years ago.

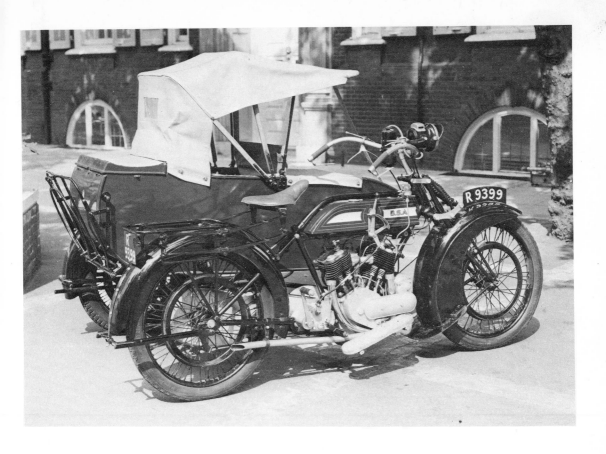

BSA, 1922   Great Britain

DURING the years that closely followed World War I the heavy-duty motorcycle-sidecar combination came into its own as personal transport for the working man who could not afford—and very often did not want—a car. This 1922 BSA outfit is a splendid example of the type. Most of it, including the front fork, three-speed gearbox, double-barrelled carburettor and even the chains, as well as the sidecar chassis and body, was made in the company's workshops. Only items such as the magneto (Lucas), saddle, tyres and lights were bought-out fittings. The sturdy V-twin 985cc (80mm × 98mm) engine had large diameter, interchangeable side valves. Very wide and deep mudguards and footboards protected the driver, and massive alumimium cases enclosed the chains. In addition to dummy belt-rim brakes fore and aft, there was an encased rear drum brake, cable-operated by a leftside toe-pedal. Fully laden, this heavyweight—the complete outfit scaled 600lb—could cruise effortlessly at 45-50mph and had a fuel consumption of about 55mpg. The utterly reliable 'Beeza combo', as it was popularly known, provided many thousands of happy families with the opportunity cheaply to explore their own country in the days when there was such a thing as the open road.

TO CONTEST the 1921 Senior Tourist Trophy race H. R. (later Sir Harry) Ricardo designed for Triumph a powerful ohv four-valve single-cylinder engine of the then popular long-stroke type. Its dimensions were 85mm × 88mm—499cc—and it developed 20bhp. Prototypes lapped the Brooklands track at close on 80mph. This engine, which was fitted into a machine virtually identical with the company's well-established side-valve SD model, had a Ricardo slipper piston, straightforward, exposed 90° valve gear and a hand-pump splash oiling system. Ball-bearing rockers were carried by supports cast with the iron head, which was bolted through the two top fins to the iron barrel. Rocker bearings were grease-gun lubricated.

The Isle of Man performance of this machine was good enough to justify commercial production and in road-going Type R form, with 80·5mm × 97mm, 499cc measurements, the model was exhibited at the Olympia Motorcycle Show in London. The Triumph-made gearbox provided ratios of 4·32, 7·02 and 11·72:1, a Druid front fork carried a stirrup brake and the price was £121. Later, the cylinder head was redesigned with the holding-down bolts passing right through the finning, and the exhaust pipes, instead of turning sharply downwards to pass between the crankcase and the magneto, swept forward into a silencer below the Lucas Magdyno, as shown in this picture of the 1923 model which, now at £96 10s, had a new fork and a drum brake. 'Riccy' Triumphs were made until 1926/7 and, despite questionable steering characteristics, appealed to those who could afford a fast, high-quality mount.

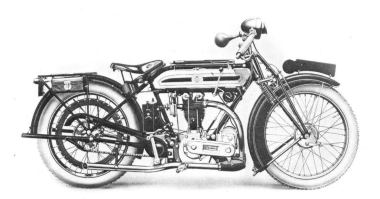

COTTON, 1923   **Great Britain**

IT WAS in 1913 that Willoughby Cotton set up the Cotton Motor Co in the city of Gloucester, and soon after he devised, originally as a 'one-off special' and fitted with the Levis twin-cylinder two-stroke engine (see page 32), a machine having a frame so uniquely successful that it remained, virtually unaltered in concept, as the backbone of a long run of highly-respected motorcycles right up to World War II.

Even when the firm was reconstituted in 1954 as E. Cotton (Motorcycles) Ltd, still at Gloucester, the then 40-year-old 'four tube' triangulated layout was re-employed. Mr Cotton's 1914-15 frame, which quickly gained a reputation for whip-free good steering, used two pairs of tubes to connect the steering head's upper and lower ends with the rear-wheel spindle lugs. A cross-brace connected them just behind the tank. The front down-tubes, chain stays and gearbox struts were also all straight members and the general set-up gave such immense vertical and lateral strength that, combined with a very low saddle, safe cornering was possible at speeds well above those of most other contemporary makes.

This virtue naturally made Cottons popular with racing men and fifth place in the 1922 Junior TT was followed by a Junior victory in 1923 when the great Irish rider, Stanley Woods (pictured) brought his Blackburne-engined mount home to collect the first of his ten Trophies. Many celebrated riders, generally using either Blackburne or JAP engines, were successful on Cottons, gaining by 1938 three IoM Trophies, four second places and three thirds, plus a host of other race, trials and record awards. In the firm's 1939 catalogue, a 150cc two-port Villiers model—still with the triangulated frame—was listed at £32.

FROM 1909 until well into the 1920s the Coventry-based Rover engineering concern, whose two-wheeler section became the New Rover Cycle Co Ltd, made very good medium-weight single- and twin-cylinder side-valve motorcycles. Then, in 1923, a breakaway came with a 250cc ohv machine. The vertical, heavily-finned 249cc (63mm × 80mm) engine had its overhead rockers mounted on ball bearings in a cast aluminium supporting structure. Ball-ended push-rods fitted into cups on the rocker arms. A rather bulky 'sump' combined the crankcase and gear housing, together with the primary and magneto drive casings. Gear changing— three speeds—was effected by a long lever mounted on the timing case. A then very up-to-date feature was the saddle tank surrounding the single top tube; also un-usual for lightweights of that period was the fitting of internal expanding brakes on both wheels. The standard model illustrated had a Brown & Barlow carburettor, an ML magneto and acetylene lighting. Prices, according to the type of lighting and other equipment fitted, ranged from £55 to £75. Rider protection was well cared for with deep front-mudguard valancing and leg-shields. A 350cc version was later listed, but production of Rover motorcycles ended after 1925.

DOT, 1923   Great Britain

AN ENTHUSIASTIC competitions rider, Harry Reed, set up in Manchester in 1903 to make a range of motorcycles that he called the D O T (Devoid of Trouble). Later, his company became Dot Motors and until quite recently a long succession of machines, using proprietary engines, were regular contenders in sporting events, During the 1920s Reed fitted many of his models with ohv oil-cooled Bradshaw engines—rather unkindly dubbed 'oil-boilers'—of 250, 350 and 500cc. The 1923 mount illustrated has the 348cc (68mm × 96mm) version. The cylinder barrel was machined inside and out and had no fins, being surrounded by an aluminium-alloy jacket cast in one with the leftside half of the crankcase. A mechanical pump, drawing from the $2\frac{1}{2}$ pint sump, kept the jacket filled with oil while the engine was running. On a 4·9:1 compression ratio, 11bhp was developed at 3,600rpm. The cast-iron, well-finned, detachable head carried a rocker box that left only the ends of the arms exposed. A large, vertical tube enclosed the pushrods. Less magneto and carburettor, the engine weighed 54lb. General specification included a Moss three-speed gearbox, BTH magneto, Binks carburettor, saddle tank and drum brakes. Weight was 200lb and the price £57 10s.

FOR over fifty years in the top rank of the world's motorcycle makers, Munich-based BMW (Bayerische Motoren Werke) built their first machine in 1920. Very different from the aero engines they had previously been supplying to the Imperial German Air Force, it was a moped-type, single-cylinder two-stroke called the Flink. This was followed by the Helios, a side-valve flat-twin with a close resemblance to the Douglas that had been a great favourite with British army dispatch riders. Then, in 1922, BMW acquired the property of the near-by Bayerische Flugzeugwerke aircraft factory, and with the deal came an outstanding designer, Max Friz. It was he who, in 1923, laid out the transverse, horizontally opposed, twin-cylinder-plus-shaft-drive design that has distinguished BMW to this day.

Friz's first machine was a 500cc side-valver in unit construction with a three-speed gearbox, flywheel and car-type clutch. The propellor-shaft drove the rear wheel through a crownwheel and pinion assembly that constituted part of the otherwise tubular frame, and a leaf-spring front fork was reminiscent of the Indian system. A front drum brake was used (not in this picture of the prototype, which shows a friction damper modification) and there was direct pedal application of a shoe to the rear dummy belt-rim. The BMW carburettor had double barrels, one controlling the fuel and the other the air intake. A combined magneto-dynamo supplied current for the lights and horn. Producing some 8bhp at 3,300rpm, the R 32 weighed 270lb and was the forerunner of over fifty different model types that included ohvs (from 1925), racing ohcs (1936), 500, 600 and 750cc capacities, pressed-steel and tube frames,

plunger (1936) and pivot (1955) rear suspension—and the world's first oil-damped, telescopic front fork (1935). From 1925 until 1967 BMW also built single-cylinder models in 200, 250, 300 and 400cc categories, all having shaft drive and with general specifications that kept pace with the development of their bigger brothers.

SUNBEAM, 1924   Great Britain

AFTER many years of successfully making very high-quality bicycles, John Marston Ltd, of Wolverhampton, went into motorcycle production in 1912 and immediately set such impressive standards of design, engineering and finish that ownership of a 'Marston 'beam' marked a man as one of a band of connoisseurs with exclusive and expensive tastes. The firm's first powered machine was a 2¾hp two-speeder and chief among a number of then advanced features was all-chain drive, fully enclosed in dust-excluding, oil-tight cases—a direct reproduction of the unique 'little oilbath' arrangement that characterised the pedal cycles. A 500cc single, as well as several differently-engined twins, followed but the 350cc side-valve Sunbeam held its appeal for many years, even for a long period after overhead valves were introduced in 1923.

The 1924 machine illustrated shows the long-stroke 347cc (70mm × 90mm) Roadster model at the height of its popularity. Priced at £78 5s, it had a three-speed Sunbeam gearbox with cross-over drive, mechanical oil pump, AMAC carburettor, new-style front fork, dummy belt-rim brakes and footboards. Smooth-running, quiet and comfortable, it was a delightful machine to drive and maintain, the 'everlasting' quality of the enamelling and plating and steadfast reliability contributing to an investment value never surpassed by any other type of motorcycle.

45

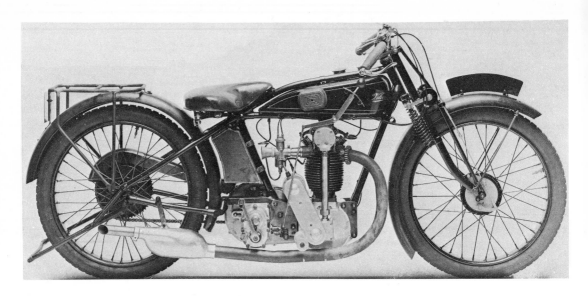

SIRE of a long and highly-successful line of sports and racing single-cylinder ohc machines, the mount illustrated was the prototype of the Model K 350cc Velocette, of which three were built in 1924/5. It was conceived by Percy Goodman, the elder of the company founder's two engineer sons, and he set out to produce a fast, reliable four-stroke to complement the long-established two-stroke range. The design, undergoing innumerable development modifications although remaining fundamentally unchanged, continued in production until 1948, when Veloce Ltd finally dropped the road-going 'cammy' models from the catalogue. A list of the famous riders who, during that era, won competition laurels on these sleek, black beauties would read like a motorcyclists' 'Who's Who.'

Percy Goodman's original specification included a 348cc (74mm × 81mm) cylinder with near-90° valves rocker-operated from a single camshaft, bevel-driven via a splined vertical shaft. Except for the outer ends of

the rocker arms, the overhead gear was all-enclosed. A pump on the leftside end of the camshaft drew oil from a compartment in the wedge-shaped tank, the spillage from the cam-box draining down the vertical shaft tube to the engine base on the constant-loss principle. As with the two-stroke, the primary chain (enclosed) was located inside the final drive, this method allowing for a narrow, rigid crankcase. A three-speed gearbox, actually a modified version of the two-stroke type, was used. Extensive testing included entries by the works' tester, Fred Povey, in such diverse events as the Colmore Trial and the Junior TT.

When the Model K went into production in 1925, lubrication was altered to the dry-sump system with a separate tank and a mainshaft-driven pump; the magneto chain-case ceased to have parallel sides and became lozenge-shaped, as it remained thereafter; and the front brake back-plate gained a water-excluding apron. Oldham couplings replaced the splines in the camshaft drive. The price was £65. Later in the year a guaranteed 80mph Super Sports version, the KSS, was introduced at £75 and in 1928, after Alec Bennettt's Junior TT victory, a racing replica, the ever-famous KTT, was marketed. This model was the first-ever 'off-the-shelf' TT replica to go into continuous production.

HENDERSON, 1924 U.S.A.

THE history of the Henderson, one of the most famous of four-cylinder motorcycles, is involved. It was in 1911 that Glaswegian W. G. 'Bill' Henderson set up a business in Rochester, NY, to make and market his own design of machine which had its four separate, air-cooled cylinders in line and with overhead inlet valves. The original 1,068cc capacity was later increased to 1,168cc and a reverse gear supplemented the three forward speeds in the unit construction gearbox. In 1917 Henderson, who had moved, first to Detroit and then to Cleveland, sold his company to the Schwinn-Excelsior concern of Chicago, but he continued with that firm for two years before leaving to form the ACE Motor Corporation in Philadelphia, where he produced the four-cylinder Ace machine that eventually became the Indian Ace, latterly called the Indian Four.

Meanwhile, Arthur Lemon had developed the Henderson at Chicago, along with the other Schwinn products, the V-twin Excelsior and Super-X models. The 11·5hp 1924 Henderson pictured had a 1,301cc (68·2mm × 89mm) side-valve engine, Zenith carburettor, Simms gear-driven magneto, dynamo lighting, spiral bevels in the gearbox, leading-link front fork and a noise-reducing brake on the camshaft. Its price in Britain was £137. The picture shows the typical American method of clutch control by rocking pedals and the leftside gear control; the shorter of the two levers operated the reverse gear. With various modifications and improvements, Henderson fours were produced until 1931.

LIKE the Model P Triumph and the EW Douglas, the 250cc 'round tank' BSA was one of those milestones in motorcycle design that won fame on its value-for-money appeal. When it was announced in January 1924, this likeable lightweight was priced at £39 10s, less lights, and it quickly established itself as a hard-working, trouble-free, fuel miser. For a number of years up to 1923, BSA had not listed any four-strokes smaller than 500cc. Then, in that year, a side-valve 350cc version of the half-litre type was introduced. But the 250 was an entirely new conception, although in certain respects it resembled an experimental quarter-litre two-stroke machine built in 1922, but never marketed.

The 1924 'round tank' model had a side-valve 249cc (63mm × 80mm) engine of simple design with a roller bearing big-end and a flat-top aluminium piston. The magneto platform-bracket was cast in one with the rightside crankcase half and one of the wheels in the mag gear train drove a mechanical oil pump housed in the casing. An enclosed primary chain linked with a constant-mesh two-speed gear, the ratios of which were 6·25 and 11·66:1. Customers living in hilly country could order lower gearing of 6·64 and 12·39:1. Braking was on the rear wheel only, by a dummy belt-rim system independently operated by pedal and handlebar lever. BSA had to go to court to prove that the arrangement was, indeed, 'independent' as the law required. Unusually small diameter—24in—wheels were used and the overall weight was 170lb. Maximum speed was in the 43-45mph bracket but, when an improved three-speed model was introduced, 50mph was well within the grasp of this lively little 'un. Fifteen thousand machines were sold in the first year and, when the production run ended some four years later, 35,000 'round tanks' had passed out of the BSA factory. A few are still going strong.

SUPER-X, 1925   U.S.A.

SUCCESSOR to the American Excelsior range, the Super-X was made by the Schwinn-owned Excelsior Manufacturing & Supply Co, of Chicago, between 1924 and 1931. A narrow-angle V-twin engine had overhead inlet valves, Schebler carburettor, a Split-dorf magneto and separate dynamo lighting. The leftside gear lever controlling the company's own three-speed box, and the rocking pedal clutch operation, were typical of American practice at that time. Two models were made, a 1,000cc and a 738cc, their general specifications differing only in the engine capacity. The 1925 mount pictured was the smaller of the two and was priced at £100, including lighting equipment and electric horn. The mechanical oil pump was located above the clutch housing and a supplementary hand-pump fed directly to the crankcase.

DURING the period 1901 to 1953, after which it became Anglicised, the famous Hendee-Indian concern, of Springfield, Mass, produced some of the finest motorcycles in the world. For power, smooth performance, reliability and long life the all-red, V-twin side-valve models of the inter-wars years, particularly the 596cc (70mm × 78mm) Scout, the 998cc Chief and the 1,234cc Big

Chief, were at the top of the American market and enjoyed wide sales in Great Britain. The 1925 Scout outfit illustrated was typical of the range. Costing £72 10s (solo), it had detachable alloy cylinder heads, enclosed valve gear, three-speed gearbox, Schebler carburettor, Splitdorf magneto, separate dynamo lighting and balloon (25in × 3·85in) tyres.

NER-A-CAR, 1925   Great Britain/U.S.A.

AN AMERICAN, Carl A. Neracher, in 1919 patented a highly unorthodox motorcycle which, because it employed a chassis in some respects resembling that of a motorcar, and because of his own surname, he called a Ner-A-Car. A company was formed at

Syracuse, New York, and a licence to build machines in England was sold to the Sheffield-Simplex Co, first based at Tinsley, Yorks, but later moved to Kingston, Surrey. British production began in 1921.

The two pressed-steel, channel-section

frame members extended from an unsprung rear fork, around the midships area, to splay outwards to allow steering movement for the front wheel, which was articulated on a coil-spring leading link passing through the hub and carrying the knuckle joint on which the wheel turned. A drag-link connected with the vertical steering column, behind which was mounted the 285cc two-stroke Sheffield-Simplex engine, with its crankshaft set longitudinally. Five-speed gearing was achieved by means of a friction disc which was moved by a rightside lever across the flat face of the flywheel, contact being maintained by spring pressure. The 'clutch', separating the friction spider from the flywheel, was cable-operated by twisting the left handlebar grip. In addition to a rear drum brake, there was also a transmission brake on the cross-shaft. A flywheel-magneto-generator provided electric lighting while under way, but acetylene 'parking' lamps were included in the original specification, when the price was £69 6s. In the 1925 form shown in the picture (with the top cowling removed to expose the 'works'), the machine weighed about 180lb, had a Binks carburettor and an HT magneto driven by chain. Towards the end of the Ner-A-Car's life, which came in 1926, sv and ohv 350cc Blackburne engines were fitted, with conventional, in-line, all-chain and three-speed gearbox transmission. Leaf-type rear springing was also devised.

THE Triumph company, while still making one of the most exclusive single-cylinder machines on the market, the four-valve Ricardo model, suddenly went to the opposite extreme and for 1925 announced a mount whose price was some 35 per cent below that of any other post-World War I motorcycle in the same category. At £42 17s 6d, the Model P Triumph caused a sensation—although there was nothing wildly exciting about its specification. It had a simple, 494cc (84mm × 89mm) side-valve engine with splash oiling. The Triumph gearbox provided ratios of 5·06, 8·2 and 14·12:1 and the only novelty was the front brake, a contracting band arrangement that was not very efficient and was discarded in favour of a conventional drum brake a year later. What attracted the customers was the combination of an ultra-low price with Triumph quality workmanship. Although the factory had been geared to low manufacturing costs, there was no skimping in either materials or in the general specification, which was entirely adequate. Great quantities of Model Ps were produced—as many as a 1,000 a week in the early stages—and they are today among the most numerous types entered in vintage runs and rallies.

COVENTRY-EAGLE, 1925   **Great Britain**

IN THE heydays of the big V-twin, the
Coventry-Eagle Flying 8 was a near-rival to
the Brough Superior, both marques using
8hp JAP engines and having impressively
wide, bulbous saddle tanks. Whereas Brough
models were distinguished by plating, the
tanks of the Flying 8s were finished in crimson
and black, with a distinctive leather covering
over the kneegrip area. The 1925 de luxe
model shown has the then-new reinforced
frame—duplicated back stays and tank tubes
—carrying a side-valve super sports twin-
camshaft engine of 976cc (85·5mm × 85mm)
with a Binks carburettor and Lucas magneto.

Magdyno electrics were optional. An un-
damped Druid fork and a three-speed
Sturmey-Archer gearbox were specified. For
such a heavy and powerful machine, the
braking was inadequate, there being only a
5in diameter drum on the front wheel and
a dummy belt-rim arrangement at the rear.
With gas lighting, the model illustrated was
priced at £145 (solo). With a single-camshaft
engine, the price was £120 (less lights).
Before the Flying 8 range was discontinued
in the early 1930s, models were available
with the 998cc ohv JAP unit.

CHATER-LEA, 1926   Great Britain

FROM 1900 Chater-Lea Ltd had been build-ing sturdy, reliable, conventional motor-cycles, a considerable proportion of the out-put being supplied to the Automobile Association's sidecar-driving road patrols. The advent, in 1926, of one of the prettiest, fastest machines of the period, the 348cc ohc Super Sports model was therefore quite a sensation—especially when Brooklands track-master Dougal Marchant, who had done the development work on the Woodman-designed engine, achieved 100mph figures in races and record attacks.

The power unit of this delightful machine was remarkable for its clean exterior appear-ance. The right half of the crankcase incorporated a smoothly-cast 'blister' carry-ing the bevels for the cam drive-shaft, which was enclosed in a tall, plated tube. Splined at both ends, this shaft drove a short, vertical camshaft, supported on ball bearings and carrying two face cams. Well finned, the aluminium cambox enclosed all the overhead gear except the extremities of the rockers, and was positively lubricated. From the separate tank, oil was drawn by a worm-type pump mounted in another 'blister' below the bevels. The pump forced oil through a pipe which ran up the hollow vertical drive shaft into the cambox, and thence back to the tank. A secondary, constant-loss splash system involv-ing a Best & Lloyd pump, driven off the magneto, took care of crankcase lubrication. A saddle tank, low-slung handlebars, a sweep-ing, big-bore exhaust pipe, a tidy lever-change for the Moss four-speed gearbox, and tommy-bar wheel nuts were other features that helped to make the face-cam Chater-Leas highly desirable property for the sports-men of the mid-1920s.

DOUGLAS, 1926   Great Britain

ANNOUNCED in September 1925 for the 1926 season, the Douglas model EW was one of those motorcycles that instantly 'rang the bell' with riders. At a remarkably low price it offered a lively performance, very good roadholding and a most attractive, aestheti-cally well-balanced appearance. As with every Douglas that had emanated from the Bristol factory, established in 1909 when the firm began making machines fitted with the Barter design of horizontally-opposed engine, it had a flat-twin unit, which was mounted lengthwise in a loop frame. Dimensions of the cylinders were 60·8mm × 60mm—348cc—and the side-valve layout was neatly com-pleted with alloy covers that matched up with the timing case-cum-magneto gear-drive assembly. Two-ring aluminium pistons were attached to H-section con-rods with roller-bearing big-ends on a built-up crank-shaft.

Transmission was through the marque's traditional flywheel clutch to a compact, three-speed gearbox with enclosed kickstarter mechanism. Gear control was by rods and a bellcrank to a lever that protruded through the blue-and-silver enamelled tank. Eight-inch diameter drum brakes were fitted with a type of self-wrapping shoe which was intended to provide a semi-servo effect. With a very low centre of gravity and an all-up weight of under 200lb, the EW handled

splendidly. The engine produced 10bhp at 4,000rpm and could run up to a sewing-machine-like 6,800rpm—over 60mph. This combination of easy riding with high engine revolutions was ultimately the EW's undoing. Because it yielded its performance so smoothly, over-enthusiastic owners tended to try to extract too much from what was, after all, no more than a 350cc side-valver, lightly built to a very low price. Complete with acetylene lighting, but less speedometer, it cost only £41 10s in the 1926 form illustrated.

AFTER a production run of some twenty years, the Coventry-based Rudge-Whitworth company dropped its Multi models around 1925. A Senior TT winner in 1914, this famous type used a unique direct belt-drive transmission system whereby a progressively variable range of gearing, between 3·5 and 7 : 1, was achieved by means of an expanding-contracting pulley on the engine shaft and a similarly adjustable belt-rim on the rear wheel, the operation being so arranged that the belt was always in line. The Rudge Multi, which was the first 500cc machine to cover sixty miles in one hour at Brooklands Track, had its pushrod-operated inlet valve directly over the side exhaust valve.

The Multi's 85mm × 89mm, 499cc, dimensions were retained when, in 1926, the firm produced its highly successful four-valve, four-speed model (illustrated). Disposed east-west fashion, the solid steel pushrods operated a pair of double-pronged rockers, each of which depressed two valves set in a pent-roof cylinder head. The inlet ports were siamesed into one manifold; the separate exhaust ports were parallel. Using pegs instead of dogs for top and bottom gear engagement, so making

for short, stiff shafts, the constant-mesh gearbox was one of the sturdiest, most reliable units of its period, providing three close-ratio general purpose gears with an emergency 'low'. The company's patented system of proportionately coupled rim-brakes was claimed to be the ultimate in safe stopping, allowing full power to be applied without either wheel locking.

The Standard model shown was continued into 1928 (with a revised exhaust pipe layout and an internal oil pump), when it was joined by the immediately popular Special and Sports editions with splayed (40°) exhaust ports, straight top tubes, saddle tanks and 8in × 1½in coupled drum brakes. All models had wheels that were quickly detachable and interchangeable—even with a sidecar. The advertised speeds and prices of these fine machines, the forerunners of winners of TTs and many other international and national competition successes, including 200 miles in two hours at Brooklands, were, in 1928, Standard (15bhp), 60mph, £46; Special (18bhp), 70mph, £55; Sports (20bhp), 85mph, £60. A 6-volt ML Maglita lighting set added £5 5s to the cost.

A WATER-COOLED, inclined, side-by-side twin two-stroke engine; an open, straight-tube, triangulated frame; telescopic front fork; all-chain-drive; two-speed gear—and the first-ever kickstarter—all these features were embodied in one uniquely designed motor-cycle as far back as 1908. This was the Scott, product of the fertile brain of a Bradford, Yorks, dyer's technician, Alfred Angas Scott, who, since 1902, had experimented with two-cycle type petrol engines for boat and bicycle propulsion. His extra-ordinarily advanced machine, with its smooth, 'four-cylinder' torque, light weight and low centre of gravity, was so successful in competitions such as hill-climbs that organisers handicapped it! After a brief period of production in the Jowett car factory at Idle, Bradford, the Scott company moved to Shipley and remained there until the factory closed in 1950, after which production was carried on into the 1960s by a Birmingham firm of jig and tool makers.

The 1926 Flying Squirrel depicted—still a flyer in the hands of its present owner, racer-trialsman Sammy Miller—represents the marque at the height of its career. Subsequent efforts to keep up with the times brought elaboration and overweight that militated against the Scott's most attractive virtues—its squirrel-like agility and its utter simplicity. The 498cc (68·25mm × 68·25mm) engine has a 180° crankshaft with overhung crankpins and an 'open' flywheel between the two crankcases (imagine a bicycle crank assembly with the chainwheel as the fly-wheel and the pedals as crankpins). Roller-bearing mains and big-ends are used and lubrication is direct by a Pilgrim pump, in this case driven off the magneto. Oil is carried in a compartment in the fuel tank which is the 1924 TT-type variation on the original oval-shaped drum carried on the seat pillar. Gearing is by two chains from mainshaft to countershaft, engagement being made by metal-to-metal clutches operated by a rocking HI-LO pedal. There is no hand clutch control. Ratios are 3·75 and 5·4:1. The magneto, as well as the rear wheel, is driven from the countershaft, which has a ratchet mechanism connected by bicycle chain to the kickstart pedal. The mount pictured has air-cooled cylinder heads, only the barrels being water-jacketed. A lengthening of the stroke to 74·6mm produced a 596cc version which was much favoured by sidecar enthusiasts.

FOUNDED in Coventry in 1900, the Rex Motor Manufacturing Co Ltd built up in the early days of motorcycling a reputation that was second to none. Rex machines, in single-cylinder and V-twin forms, were well designed, well built and immensely popular. In 1922 the firm amalgamated with another pioneer concern, the Coventry Acme Motor Co Ltd, to form the Rex-Acme Motor Manufacturing Co Ltd. Although many types of proprietary engines were used, Rex-Acme mounts chiefly owed their fame to the ohv Blackburne units. It cannot be said that there was anything revolutionary in the design of these mounts, practically the only components made by the company were the frames. But they handled extremely well and had a clean, business-like look about them that appealed to the sports riders of the 1920s.

There can be no doubt that their sales success was largely due to Walter Handley who, after a couple of years racing OK machines, transferred his allegiance to Rex-Acme, later becoming a director of the company. Between 1924 and 1930, Handley rode Rex-Acmes in fourteen TT races (in all solo classes from the Ultra-lightweight to the Senior), being three times winner, never finishing in lower than third place and setting up four fastest laps. The 1927 machine illustrated is today as good as it was forty-six years ago and is one of the last of the line from the Rex-Acme factory, for production ceased in 1928. An attempt in 1932 by the next-door Mills-Fulford sidecar company to revive the marque was unsuccessful. The TT sports type shown has a Blackburne engine of 71mm × 88mm, 348cc, wet-sump lubrication by Pilgrim pump, a Burman three-speed gearbox, diamond frame with duplicated chain stays, Webb front fork and a registration index that would have been perfect had the letters been transposed. The original price in Britain was £60.

AJS, 1927   **Great Britain**

ALTHOUGH they had for several years been
making petrol engines for other manufacturers, the five Stevens brothers, of Wolverhampton, did not build an AJS motorcycle
until 1909. Their very successful design of
350cc side-valve machine gained first and
second places in the 1914 Junior TT. In
1920, an ohv racing version was constructed
and was immediately another TT winner.
It had cylinder dimensions of 74mm ×
81mm, 349cc, and when the original exhaust
valve diameter, $1\frac{9}{16}$in, was increased to $1\frac{5}{8}$in,
the type became known as the 'big port'.
(In 1924 AJS were the first motorcycle
makers to use an inlet valve of greater
diameter than the exhaust, $1\frac{11}{16}$in and $1\frac{1}{2}$in
respectively.)

The racing specials were ridden by many
famous men and gained many successes

leading to the arrival, in 1926, of the chaindrive ohc 'cammy Ajays.' It was in 1923 that
an ohv production version of the 'big port'
was launched. It had the same bore and
stroke measurements and employed the
original AJS method of holding down the
cylinder barrel by two long bolts and a yoke
across the vertically-finned head. The plates
carrying the exposed rocker gear were also
typical, those in this picture of the 1927 H6
model being solid and not 'fret-worked' as
with earlier engines. Duralumin rockers, an
aluminium piston, $1\frac{5}{8}$in tulip valves, double-
row roller bearing big-end, mechanical pump
lubrication and friction damped front fork
were features. The model illustrated was
priced at £53. A 498cc (84mm × 90mm)
version—the company's first ohv 500—was
introduced in 1926.

WHEN the P & M company launched its lightweight Panthette model in 1927 it was seen that its designer, Granville Bradshaw, had not abandoned his belief in the transverse twin–gearbox unit, as exemplified in his 1919 ABC layout. For the Panthette, however, he inclined the cylinders at an included angle of 60° and he chose a capacity of 246cc (50mm × 61·5mm). He still favoured pushrod-operated overhead valves but this time had adopted an ingenious leaf-spring method of control. The laminated springs bore on the rod ends of the rockers, whose opposite ends were forked to engage with collars on the stems. Thus it was the rocker itself that not only opened the valve but also pulled it back onto its seat. This quasi-desmodromic arrangement also provided a push-rod return-spring effect.

All the valve gear was fully enclosed, there being curved aluminium plates covering the rocker boxes, which were cast integrally with the iron barrels. A magneto-driving cam-shaft, lying between the cylinders, was geared to the crankshaft which passed the drive through a multi-plate clutch to the gearbox (ratios, 5·4, 7·3, 10·7 and 15·8:1). Spiral bevels drove a cross-shaft carrying the rightside sprocket. Gears were shifted by a car-type lever. Flat, strip-steel members formed a cradle around the power unit and were bolted at their upper ends to an I-section forged 'backbone' that incorporated the steering head. The saddle-and-chain stays assembly was of conventional tube type. In its time the smallest multi on the market, the machine weighed 250lb (engine weight 76lb). Maximum speed was about 55mph and the price was £50, an incredibly low figure for a mount that involved so much workmanship. A sports model, differing chiefly in having a more eyeable exhaust system, was subsequently offered, but not many Panthettes left the Cleckheaton works and those that have survived are very rare creatures.

HUMBER, 1927   Great Britain

ONE of the oldest, and at one time the largest, producers of motorcycles in Britain, Humber Ltd, Coventry, had marketed from 1900 all sorts of different models with various engine sizes, in single- and twin-cylinder forms, when, in 1923, it was decided to concentrate on a 350cc side-valve pattern. An ohv version followed shortly and at the Olympia Show in 1927 an ohc edition made its appearance.

The ohc model was built very much on the same lines as the ohv type and had the same engine dimensions, 75mm × 97mm, 349cc. However, the entirely new design of cylinder head had twin exhaust ports, heavily ribbed. Bevel drive was used for the enclosed vertical shaft, the 2:1 reduction being at the upper end. The camshaft was ball-bearing-mounted in a large aluminium housing and only the outer ends of the rockers, carrying the adjustable tappets, were exposed. A simple gear-type pump on the cambox drew oil from a compartment within the main tank and delivered it, on the constant-loss principle, through two pipes, one to the crankcase and one to the cam gear, whence the overflow passed down the vertical shaft tube to the engine base. Plain bearings supported the mainshaft and there were double-row, roller-bearing races in the big-end. Humber made the three-speed gearbox, controlled by a lever on the good-looking saddle tank which was panelled in blue on a black background. First priced at £60, the ohc Humber went through some minor modifications before the company turned to a 'cars only' policy in 1930.

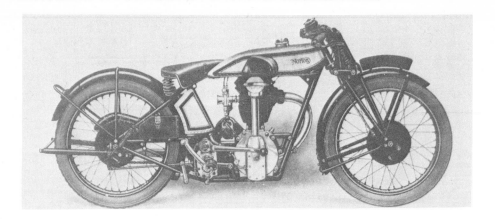

IT WAS in 1922 that the Norton company, whose side-valve Brooklands Specials had gained innumerable race and record successes, adopted overhead valves. Two years later, a Model 18 push-rod-engined 500cc Norton won the Senior TT. This was the first Trophy gained by the marque, for Rem Fowler's historic victory, on a Peugeot-engined Norton in the twin-cylinder class of the 1907 first-ever TT, entitled him to a silver rose bowl, which he never received. Alec Bennett, the 1924 winner, was again victorious in 1927, this time on an overhead camshaft Norton. For racing or roadburning, this type was offered as the Model CS1 and the mount illustrated is the 1927 Olympia Show exhibit, costing £89.

The model designation stood for 'cam shaft one,' and the early examples became known as the 'cricket bat' types on account of the shape of the timing chest and the vertical cam-drive shaft. As well as a new engine, the CS1 had a new cradle frame and Norton's first saddle tank. The long-familiar 79mm × 100mm, 490cc, cylinder measurements were used and the 'bottom half' was almost the same as that of the ohv types, which

were themselves based on the original side-valvers. The timing chest contained the lower pair of cam-drive bevels and a double-plunger pump for the dry-sump lubrication system. The 2 : 1 reduction between the lower and upper pairs of bevels was shared so that the vertical shaft ran at a lower-than-engine speed.

Two cams on a single shaft operated two-piece rockers which had hardened steel pads as cam followers and screw-and-locknut adjusters over the exposed valve stems. There was positive oil feed to the cambox. To allow the sweeping pipe to clear the front down-tube the exhaust port was offset to the left. A platform behind the cylinder barrel carried the magneto, which was chain-driven from the engine shaft. A three-speed Sturmey-Archer gearbox had foot control by a long lever directly mounted on the box. Positive-stop pedal operation had not then been invented. These fast, handsome machines (a 348cc CJ—Cam-shaft Junior—model was introduced a year later) were superb roadholders and were the foundation of long-lasting Norton supremacy in single-cylinder road racing.

SOON after the end of World War I two Coventry engineering families came together in motorcycle manufacture in a factory in Lower Ford Street, where Excelsior machines had once been made. Gordon Francis, from Lea-Francis, joined with the Barnetts, who had formerly had a hand in Singers and later made Invicta lightweights, to build conventional diamond-framed Francis-Barnett motorcycles. In 1923 Gordon Francis put into practice an idea he had while serving in the army—and produced the 'built like a bridge' triangulated frame that was to distinguish 'Fanny-Bs' for many years. This simple layout, built up with lengths of straight tube (all of which could be stowed in a golf-bag) was tremendously strong, cheap to make and easy to assemble—two men could bolt it up in twenty mintues.

The first models had 147cc Villiers two-stroke engines with Albion two-speed gearboxes and chain-cum-belt transmission. They were priced at £27. A number of different types and makes of engine were subsequently carried in this frame without very much change to its original design. In 1925, a 346cc side-valve JAP model was introduced and in 1928 F & B installed the 344cc (57·15mm × 67mm) Villiers twin-cylinder two-stroke unit and called the model the Pullman (pictured).

The fore-and-aft unit had the flywheel magneto mounted forward of the crankcase, which also housed the worm-gear-driven three-speed assembly operated by a car-type lever. A link-pattern front fork, similar to that introduced for the 350 JAP machine, allowed the use of a really good front brake —something that had not been possible with the original front suspension which had used a pivoting arrangement controlled by a C-spring. A delightfully smooth-running, lively machine costing £65, the Pullman had one unusual hazard—a flame blowback through the carburettor could set light to the rider's left trouser leg!

FROM the drawing board of rider-designer Cyril Pullin, and made by the Ascot Motor Manufacturing Co Ltd, of Letchworth, Herts, the Ascot-Pullin created a sensation when it began its short life in October 1928. This was in a period when it was widely believed that the motorcycle of the future would be a 'car on two wheels' and, among the several engineers who endeavoured to achieve this aim, Pullin probably got closest to the target.

His machine embodied fifty-two 'special features,' listed among them being the pressed-steel frame, fork blades and handlebar; compensated 8in diameter hydraulic brakes; an automatic prop-stand using telescopic plungers; an adjustable damper on the enclosed front-fork spring; quickly detachable, interchangeable wheels; enclosed rear chain with quick adjustment; several oil filters; control cable tensioning by knurled thumbscrews on the levers; $4\frac{1}{2}$gal

fuel and $1\frac{1}{4}$gal oil tanks; a fourway petrol tap, incorporating a filter, with On, Off, Drain and Reserve ($1\frac{1}{2}$gal) positions; contents' gauges built into the filler caps; enclosed speedometer drive; mudproof hubs; a carrier; pillion footrests; and three toolbags.

The electrical equipment included head and tail lamps, horn and a BTH combined magneto-dynamo with a cut-out. The lights switch was fitted in a handlebar facia panel, along with ammeter, clock, speedometer and oil-pressure gauge. The two-port ohv 496cc (82mm × 94mm) engine was horizontal and in unit construction with the three-speed gearbox, the clutch running at engine speed and driving through stub-tooth gears (1:2.31 ratio) to the gearbox mainshaft. Two inclined-face transmission shock absorbers were used, one on each side of the gearbox. With vernier adjustment, the valves were operated by totally-enclosed pushrods and rockers on ball bearings. The only plain bearing in the whole machine was the con-rod little-end. Double-row caged rollers were used in the big-end. The blue and white finish of this remarkable motorcycle was in cellulose enamel. Two models were listed, the Sports Utility (pictured) and the Utility de Luxe, the latter having extra equipment, such as a two-piece telescopic windscreen, legshields and footboards. Despite all this luxury, a claimed 'honest 70mph', 150mpg and a basic price of £75, the Ascot-Pullin failed to catch on and production ended after only two seasons.

RALEIGH, 1929   Great Britain

THIS 350cc two-port Raleigh Sports model was introduced in 1929, being based on an earlier 496cc type. Except for cylinder dimensions and gear ratios, the models were practically identical and, as with all machines emanating from the famous Nottingham factory—which had first made motorcycles in the period 1899-1906—most of the main components were 'own-make.' When the company re-entered the motorcycle market in 1919 it had acquired the Sturmey-Archer gearbox patents. Side-valve flat- and V-twins up to 800cc were made, as well as singles ranging from 175 to 500cc.

The ohv engines owed much to the influence of designer-rider D. R. O'Donovan, who transferred from Norton to Raleigh in the late 1920s. Cylinder measurements were 79mm × 101mm, 496cc, for the larger machine and 71mm × 88mm for the 348cc type. Enclosed overhead rocker gear (exposed springs) was carried on steel plates bolted to the cylinder head. An aluminium piston was fitted and lubrication was by sight-feed pump from a separate tank, with a reserve hand-pump. Under the Sturmey-Archer trademark these engines were also marketed as proprietary units, being used by British (eg, Dunelt and Coventry-Eagle) and Continental makers. Capable of useful speed tuning, they were raced in many events, with factory teams in the TT. The 350cc Raleigh motorcycle weighed 315lb and in 1929 cost £53, without lights. The company ceased motorcycle production in the early 1930s but returned to the field after World War II with a variety of moped and ultra-lightweight machines.

65

IN 1920 Dunford and Elliott Ltd, of Bath Street, Birmingham, came up with a fresh idea in two-stroke motorcycle engine design. Not only was an unusual principle involved but, for the first time, motorcyclists were offered a practical single-cylinder, valveless unit with a capacity of 500cc. Indeed, this Dunelt model was the only British half-litre two-stroke single ever to be sold in quantity production. The novelty in the engine lay in the design of the piston and cylinder, whereby a supercharging effect was obtained in transferring the gas from the crankcase to the combustion chamber. This was achieved by using a piston having two diameters, a portion of the base of the skirt, carrying one ring, being considerably 'wider' than the two-ring lands above the gudgeon pin. The barrel was, of course, counter-bored to accept the double-diameter piston. This arrangement displaced 50 per cent more gas charge than could be naturally accommodated in the crankcase. As a result, not only was the combustion chamber more efficiently charged, but better exhaust scavenging was obtained, for the force of the ingoing charge drove out the exhaust gases. It was claimed that between 10 and 15 per cent more efficiency was thereby achieved. Improved cooling of the ports was another outcome of the system.

Over a period of nearly ten years, 500cc 'supercharged' Dunelts had many adherents, taking part in all types of competitions and gaining a sixth place in the 1925 Sidecar TT. For 1926, a 249cc version was produced and the half-litre model was later allowed to lapse. From 1929 the double-diameter piston was of bi-metal construction, having an iron band cast onto the upper, two-ring part of the aluminium component. This was said to retain the advantages of alloy while allowing for closer clearances, elimination of slap, reduction of ring-groove wear and freedom from sticking rings. A detachable aluminium cylinder head was a feature. The crankshaft was a solid steel forging with balance weights bolted on after con-rod assembly. The shaft ran on ball bearings and carried an outside flywheel. The 1929 K Royal de luxe 250cc model illustrated cost £47 15s with electric lighting, and a stock machine of this type gained a Double 12-Hours world's record.

BROUGH SUPERIOR, 1930   Great Britain

FIRST manufacturer to offer a guaranteed 100mph roadgoing motorcycle was George Brough—in 1924. And his famous 'he-man's choice' SS100 models were for many years at the pinnacle of a legendary range of magnificent Brough Superior machines, all in the high-power, high-quality, high-price market. Mostly these mounts were assemblies of already well-proven proprietary components, either built by Brough under licence, or built for him to special specification. For example, his engines, mainly JAP or Matchless, were individually constructed to his order. The Sturmey-Archer gearboxes, although more or less standard in appearance, were in fact extra-heavy-duty units made only for his powerful machines. His suspension systems were fabricated in the factory at Nottingham, the Castle bottom-link front fork being to Harley-Davidson pattern and the rear pivot arrangement was based on a Bentley & Draper patent. All this, combined with massively rigid main frames, and the most

impressively handsome tanks ever devised, resulted in truly 'Superior' mounts, the seal on the superiority being set by the many distinguishing touches of refinement that helped the marque to earn the title 'the Rolls Royce of motorcycles.'

The immaculately-restored example, here pictured, of the Overhead 680 member of the Black Alpine range was first registered in February 1930. It has an ohv JAP 70mm × 88mm, 678cc, engine with roller bearings for practically every revolving spindle, including the overhead and timing-case rockers. The shrouded magneto is bevel-driven and lubrication is by Pilgrim pump. The gearbox provides four speeds, the carburettor is a special Amal and 8in diameter Enfield brakes are fitted. With electric lights, horn and speedometer, the price was £110 in rigid-frame form, rear springing adding £10. An 8 to 80mph top-gear performance was claimed and fuel consumption was in the region of 80mpg.

WITHIN a year of each other, two most unusual designs of machine were announced by Matchless Motor Cycles (Colliers) Ltd, the London-based manufacturer (later Associated Motor Cycles) which had been one of Britain's biggest producers since the turn of the century. In 1929 came the Silver Arrow and, in 1930, the Silver Hawk (pictured). Except for their engines they were almost identical machines, having rear suspension on the pivoted, triangulated fork principle and pedal interconnection for the 8in diameter brakes. The power unit of the Arrow was a 397cc (54mm × 86mm) side-valve twin with the cylinders in line in one block at an angle of 26°. The one-piece cylinder head was detachable and the car-type camshaft, running in oil, drove the magneto, or Magdyno, from its rear end. A dry-sump lubrication system included a 6 pint tank mounted at the foot of the front down-tube. A Sturmey-Archer gearbox provided ratios of 5·9, 7·8, 10·4 and 17·5:1.

Weighing 308lb and on a compression ratio of 5·6 : 1, the Arrow's speed was in the 60–65mph band, and petrol consumption was of the order of 100mpg. The basic price, without extras, was £55. An easy starter, and a quiet and gentle machine to drive, the Arrow appealed mainly to solo tourists.

Its super-sports brother, the Silver Hawk, introduced in October 1930, offered much more power and punch. A 593cc (50·8mm × 73mm) four-cylinder, overhead camshaft unit, it had the same 26° angle between the cylinders, which were arranged in double-V formation in one block, with air spaces around the barrels. A two-throw crankshaft was supported on three main bearings—plain phosphor-bronze journals at the ends and rollers in the centre. A single-piece head carried the all-enclosed rocker gear, driven by a right side vertical shaft, from the base of which was taken the drive to a Lucas dynamo-coil unit incorporating the distributor. Weight of the complete machine without extras was 370lb; maximum speed on a compression ratio of 6·1:1 was 80–85mph; consumption, 75–80mpg. Only one, de luxe, model was listed and the price, £75, included a gearbox-driven speedometer, electric lights and horn, and a handlebar instrument panel. In 1930 the Silver Hawk Matchless was the only four-cylinder, rear-sprung machine in the world.

COVENTRY-EAGLE, 1930   Great Britain

A PRACTICAL breakaway from orthodox frame construction was seen in the range of Coventry-Eagle Silent Superb two-stroke machines that enjoyed a long run of popularity in the late 1920s and early 1930s. The 'chassis' consisted of two channelled pressings welded together to form the steering head. Midships rigidity was obtained through a bolted-in engine-gearbox sub-unit. This unit, complete with the dynamo and exhaust box, could be removed by withdrawing the securing bolts and disconnecting the controls. Virtually unbreakable and relatively cheap to mass produce, this frame gave a comfortable riding position and was easy to clean. The front fork blades were also steel pressings.

When first exhibited at the 1927 Olympia Show, the prototype was indeed a showpiece, for it was displayed in duralumin and polished steel; but production models had enamelled steel members. Engines were remarkably quiet, there being an expansion box forward of the crankcase and leading into large, fish-tailed silencers. Originally two Villiers flywheel-magneto-engined models were listed—a 147cc type with a two-speed Albion gearbox at £27 15s, and a 172cc three-speeder at £36 15s. Later, 250cc versions were added and the 1930 two-port Model M5 pictured included a Miller dynamo lighting set, electric horn, legshields, well-valanced mudguards and two large toolboxes. Commendable features on a machine costing only £36 were polished aluminium casings for the primary and dynamo chain drives.

HUSQVARNA, 1930

FROM Sweden's national arms factory, Husqvarna motorcycles have been produced since 1903, at first using foreign engines such as the Belgian FN, but later with units of their own design and manufacture. Apart from times of war, there has been no break in output and a wide variety of 'Husky' types have been marketed—along with other non-military products like bacon slicers and sausage machines. In the 1930s, when side-valve 550 and 1,000cc V-twins and JAP and Sturmey-Archer-engined singles were being made, Husqvarna Wapenfabriks went into international road-racing with sleek, swift 350 and 500cc pushrod ohv V-twins designed by its celebrated engineer, Folke Mannersteadt, and the 1934 mount pictured is the one Stanley Woods rode in the Senior TT of that year.

Extremely light—much alloy metal, such as Elektron, was used—its engine had a JAP/New Imperial look about it, with enclosed rocker gear and exposed hairpin valve springs. Location of the rear exhaust pipe on the left side was a distinctive feature and evidence of the designer's appreciation of the value of gas extractor effect is seen in the equal-length pipes. The front fork had rebound check springs, owing something to AJS, and the scalloped edge to the base of the petrol tank was in the then Norton pattern. Husqvarna participation in sports motorcycling today is concentrated on motocross and trials, with highly successful two-strokes from 125 to 450cc, and on speedway with other machines.

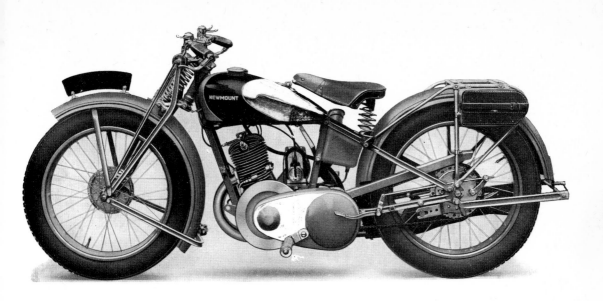

NEWMOUNT, 1930   Great Britain/Germany

AN INGENIOUS frame characterized the 300cc Newmount, which arrived in Britain from Germany in 1929 for the 1930 season. The Newmount Trading Co Ltd had been formed in Coventry to import and market certain Zündapp machines made in Munich. Carrying the Newmount tank transfer, they were fitted with such British equipment as Dunlop tyres, Renold chains and Miller electrics. The 300cc (68mm × 82·5mm, 298cc) model illustrated had an inclined two-stroke unit, with outside flywheel, which was carried in a

frame that had a drop-forged steel steering-head-cum-backbone, all the other members being bolted-on I-section forgings, fully interchangeable from one side of the machine to the other—including the front fork blades. Light, strong and reliable, this machine cost £47 10s with chain-driven magneto or Miller 6 volt coil ignition. Newmounts with Rudge Python four-valve 350 and 500cc engines were later offered, but the company disappeared after 1933.

NEW HUDSON, in the motorcycle business since 1909, was one of those Midland engineering works that liked to make things big, strong and practically everlasting. Just as the company's boardroom furniture was massive in solid mahogany, so were its side-valve motorcycles bulky in cast iron and heavy-gauge steel. Without any notable success, New Hudsons had contested the TT since 1911, but a change came when, in 1926, speed wizard Bert le Vack moved into the Birmingham factory. The ohv models built under his guidance were definitely swift. Riding them himself, he broke a number of world records and then, in 1927, Scotsman Jimmy Guthrie gained the marque a second place in the Senior TT, yielding only to the then almost unbeatable Alec Bennett.

A change of policy came in 1930 when a range of semi-enclosed mounts was evolved. These were a side-valve 547cc (83·5mm × 100mm), and two-port ohv 346cc (70mm × 90mm) and 496cc (79·5mm × 100mm) machines with their dry-sump power units inclined in duplex-tube frames. Below cylinder-barrel level side panels and an undershield completely enclosed the crankcase, magneto, dynamo and four-speed Moss gearbox. 'The result,' wrote *The Motor Cycle*, 'is a machine commendably free from nooks and crannies, one that is smart in appearance, really easy to clean and has . . . its working parts properly protected from the elements.' Despite all this and a wealth of auxiliary equipment, the new-look New Hudsons were slow sellers—basic prices ranged from £45 for the standard side-valve model to £58 10s for the specially-tuned 500cc ohv model (illustrated) weighing 360lb and having a claimed maximum speed of 85mph. Among a number of unusual features on these unusual motorcycles were: twist-grip magneto control; a backfire-proof kickstart pedal that could act as a prop stand; and a saddle with a double seat— in wet weather the top surface could be hinged forward to provide an apron to protect the rider's abdomen. Forward-facing fork-ends allowed the rear wheel to be dropped out without disconnecting the chain or upsetting adjustment.

NEW IMPERIAL, 1932   Great Britain

FIRST marketed in 1932, the New Imperial Models 16 (350cc) and 17 (500cc) combined practically all the design features that were in demand by the very large number of motorcyclists who, at that time, were classed as 'sporting clubmen'. The two machines were virtually identical, except for cubic capacity and gear ratios. A twin-port, inclined ohv with fully-enclosed rocker gear, the engine was in unit construction with the gearbox, the primary chain having an aluminium oilbath case. A forward extension of the crankcase contained the oil for the dry-sump lubrication system. Rather unusually, the barrel of the Amal carburettor was fitted horizontally. A 2½gal saddle tank was mounted over the firm's characteristic arrangement of duplicated top tubes and a Bentley & Draper patent pivoted rear fork was used; the girder front fork was of New Imperial's own make.

Basic price of the Model 16 was £57. Engine dimensions were 74mm × 80mm, 346cc; gear ratios were 5·4, 8·1 and 15·8:1. A touring speed of 70mph and fuel consumption of 95mpg were claimed. The Model 17, at £59 10s, had a 499cc (86mm × 86mm) engine; ratios of 5, 8 and 13:1; maximum speed of 75mph, and 90mpg. From the beginning of the century New Imperials built many different types of good motorcycles, mostly using their own components. Consistent supporters of competitions, they won six TTs between 1921 and 1936. On the retirement of the chairman, Norman Downs, in 1939, the company was sold to Ariel-Triumph chief, Jack Sangster, who planned to move production from the Birmingham factory to Coventry. In the event, that was the end of what had for nearly forty years been a much respected, go-ahead marque.

FROM time to time in the long history of motorcycling, certain machines have become landmarks on the road of development. Though long gone from production, they are still remembered vividly as the outstanding models of their respective epochs, having enjoyed instant approbation from the moment they appeared, and sustained popularity for years afterwards. Without a doubt the BSA 'Sloper', introduced in August 1926, was a leader among these classic mounts. Machines having their engines inclined forwards were nothing new, but the way in which BSA blended a robust 500cc ohv unit into a low-saddle (25in) duplex cradle frame had an immediate appeal—and led to a crop of imitations.

The Sloper had no racing development behind it, and was never intended for high-speed work, although the Super Sports version was capable of a 70–75mph gait. The main attractions of the model were its good looks, comfortable and quiet riding, comprehensive specification, easy maintenance and durability—there are still some in general use today. The 493cc (80mm × 98mm) two-port engine had a ¾gal capacity crankcase-sump with an oil-level indicator consisting of a float and projecting spindle. Transmission was via a dry-plate clutch and a three-speed gearbox with ratios of 4·4, 6 and 10:1. Internal expanding brakes were fitted on both wheels. Initially, prices were £47 10s for the Standard model and £53 for the Super Sports. Illustrated is the 1932 version, which had an I-section forged-steel 'backbone' frame member (introduced in 1930), the rounded saddle tank which replaced the original wedge-shaped component, and headlamp supports mounted on the sprung side of the fork links. The front brake could be operated together with the rear by the pedal, or independently by the handlebar lever.

SUNBEAM, 1932   Great Britain

JOHN MARSTON, father-figure of Sunbeam-land, Wolverhampton, died in 1918 and his family, believed to have been faced with formidable death duties, merged the company into the Nobel Industries organisation which, in 1926, became Imperial Chemical Industries. It was under the ICI banner that the marque achieved a notable comeback to international road racing.

Although prominent in other branches of the sport, particularly hill-climbs and sprints, the ohv models, introduced in 1923, had had no luck in the Isle of Man until 1927, when the manufacturers' team award went to a trio of 'beams with widely redesigned valve gear.

These mounts, first introduced in 1926 under the name of the Model 90 (there were also 350cc Model 80 versions), had twin-port cylinder heads which soon gained hairpin valve springs—the first on any make of motorcycle. C. J. P. Dodson won the Senior TT on a Model 90 in 1928 and again in 1929 when, for the third successive year, the

makers' award went to Sunbeam.

The 1932 Model 90 depicted represented just about the last of the line of Wolverhampton machines, production thereafter being transferred to the Collier brothers' factory at Woolwich.

Priced at £90 as a production racer, the '32 Model 90 had a twin-port ohv 493cc (80mm × 98mm) engine with enclosed rockers automatically lubricated, double hairpin springs, Amal carburettor, Lucas racing magneto, optional 7 or 9:1 compression ratio, Sunbeam close-ratio gearbox (4.6, 5.5, 6.7 and 9.6:1), interchangeable, balanced wheels, self-energising brakes, tubular, fish-tailed silencers and a 120mph speedometer. A hand gearlever, kickstarter, Magdyno lighting and racing exhaust pipes were optional fittings. As with all Wolverhampton 'beams, the very high quality of the black and gold enamelling and the bright plating was in keeping with the firm's superb engineering standards.

ROYAL ENFIELD, 1932   **Great Britain**

THROUGH a production life of some half-dozen years the Royal Enfield Model Z Cycar was a praiseworthy addition to the variety of very simple, highly economical 'mounts for the million' that many manufacturers felt certain would make fortunes in the 1930s. Apart from its very low price, the chief feature of the Cycar, introduced in 1932, was its frame, made from a single steel pressing, almost fully enclosing the engine, gearbox and transmission and providing, with its in-built leg-shields and valances, a high degree of rider-protection. The front fork blades were also pressings.

A 148cc (56mm × 60mm) single-cylinder, two-stroke engine, with a roller bearing big-end, operated on petroil mixture and had a Villiers flywheel magneto/coil lighting unit. A dry battery was supplied for parking purposes. An oil-bath enclosed primary chain connected with a hand-operated three-speed gearbox, the standard ratios of which were 7·2, 12·8 and 20:1. Enfields' own very effective drum brakes were fitted. Weighing 168lb and costing only a few pounds a year to run—after January 1935 the annual tax was only 12s and a tankful of fuel at that time cost about 1s 6d—the Cycar offered extremely cheap, reliable, clean, go-anywhere travel. It was priced at £19 19s, including electric lighting.

UNDER the control of Ing F. Janacek, Czechoslovakia's arms factory in Prague began building Jawa motorcycles in 1929. First models had rather ponderous ohv 500cc engines with unit gear construction and shaft drive. The frame was of pressed steel, fabricated under licence from the German Wanderer company. In 1930 English designer-rider George Patchett joined Jawa and in the period to 1939 (when he and Janacek left Czechoslovakia just ahead of Hitler's armies) the firm became very active in international competitions. Patchett's racing machines regularly figured in the European grands prix and lively two-strokes contested major trials, such as the International Six Days. The 1933 Senior TT machine, seen with Stanley 'Ginger' Wood aboard, had the Wanderer-type frame with a massive engine-gear unit. The hairpin-spring controlled valves were operated by pushrods on the left side. Post-war racing Jawas developed into the vertical twin ohc type. Currently the factory makes very popular two-strokes for touring, trials and moto-cross as well as ohv speedway mounts, and is allied with Czechoslovakia's other famous marque, CZ.

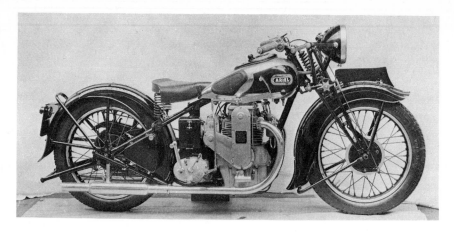

IN THE early part of 1929 there appeared an experimental prototype of a motorcycle that really was unique—and remained that way for thirty years, for no attempt was ever made by any other manufacturer to copy its clever engine design. With no name on its tanksides, that prototype machine had a 497cc (51mm × 61mm) four-cylinder engine in unit construction with a four-speed gearbox, but when it was launched as a production model later in the year its makers, Ariel Works Ltd, of Selly Oak, Birmingham, called it the Square Four and it had a separate Burman gearbox.

The 'Squariel', as it was quickly nicknamed, came from the drawing board of Edward Turner, an engineer who subsequently made many more notable contributions to both motorcycle and car development. The Square Four was so called because its cylinders were vertically disposed in the block like the legs of a square-topped table. Two geared-together 180° throw crankshafts ran on ball main bearings and the con-rods had roller-bearing big-ends. The gear teeth on the forward shaft also drove the halftime shaft from which were taken the chain drives to the overhead camshaft and

the magneto. Through a transmission shock absorber, the primary chain drive was taken from the rear shaft. One forward-facing Amal carburettor fed the intricate manifolding in the detachable head, which was equally tortuously cored to bring the exhaust gases forward into a pair of pipes. Removal of eight bolts allowed the cylinder head and rocker box to be detached without disturbance of the timing gear. In other respects the Model 4F shared a general specification with the side-valve and ohv singles.

The 1934 machine pictured was priced at £72 10s, Lucas Magdyno electric equipment costing £5 15s extra. By this time the engine capacity had been increased to 597cc (56mm × 61mm). Although the geared crankshaft principle was retained, the Square Fours were completely redesigned after 1937 as 1,000cc machines—actually 997cc, 65mm × 75mm—and pushrods replaced the ohc arrangement. Forward-facing exhaust manifolds were bolted to the sides of the head. The ohc Squariels were beautifully sweet-running machines but required careful maintenance to prevent oil leaks. The '1,000' 4G models, developing 42bhp at 5,800rpm, were equally popular either solo or with a sidecar, especially when fitted with the firm's plunger-type rear suspension. They were not dropped from production until 1959 when Ariel concentrated on a two-stroke-only range. Whoever posed the accompanying picture should have ensured that the front brake reaction-strap was properly bolted to the fork blade.

OEC, 1934   Great Britain

FROM the very earliest days to the present time, motorcycle steering design has, with only a few exceptions, followed that of the pedal cycle, depending on some kind of wheel fork with a stem swivelling on bearings in a headstock. One of the exceptions was the Ner-A-Car, already described; another equally unorthodox, was the OEC Duplex arrangement, patented in 1927 by a Gosport, Hants, firm which had been founded in 1921 as the Osborn Engineering Co and later became OEC Ltd, of Portsmouth.

The Duplex system was created to provide completely whip-free steering. A pair of rigid stanchions were joined at their bases by bowed-out extensions of the lower frame tubes. A second pair of struts were attached to the other pair by top and bottom links

mounted on substantial bearings. Turned by the handlebar, mounted on a crosspiece, the pivoting struts carried the front axle, there being spring-loaded sliding members within the tubes. Unsprung weight was reduced virtually to that of the wheel, tyre and brake. Later, OEC added rear suspension incorporating friction-damped plunger units, as shown in this view of a 1934 model powered by a 980cc JAP side-valve engine. Before going out of business in 1954, when it was making Villiers-engined lightweights, OEC had built many fine roadsters, racers and record-breakers, using JAP, Blackburne, Bradshaw, MAG, Anzani, Vulpine and their own units, as well as constructing oddities such as the enclosed, water-cooled Tinkler and the Whitwood monocar.

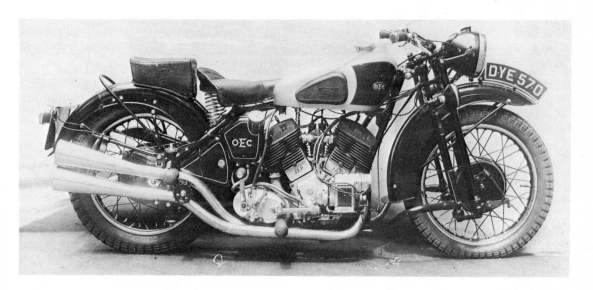

IF LOOKS could sell, the Douglas Endeavour introduced in November 1954 should have proved a bonanza for the Bristol company. And it was not just a pretty face. Designed by F. W. Dixon (note its resemblance to the Brough Superior Golden Dream, in which Freddie also had a hand), it was a practical mount, very well thought out and very well constructed. But for various reasons, not least of which was the Douglas company's financial instability at the time, the Endeavour was built only in relatively small quantities. Its transverse, side-valve 498cc (68mm × 68 mm) horizontally-opposed twin-cylinder engine lay in its robust, duplex cradle frame with the crankshaft at hub level. The housings containing the traditional Douglas engine-speed clutch and the four-speed gearbox were bolted up to the box-like crankcase. In the gearbox the mainshaft and layshaft were in the same plane, so that the propellor shaft, which in top gear ran at engine speed, was horizontally connected, through a rubber-buffer coupling, to the

bevel gear on the driving axle. The propshaft was in two parts, splined to allow simple withdrawal of the quickly detachable rear wheel.

The engine had alloy barrels with cast-iron-liners, ball main bearings and double-row duralumin-caged roller big-ends. A single, forward-facing Douglas carburettor was used and the camshaft and the Magdyno, mounted on the crankcase top, were gear driven. A four-speed gearbox had ratios of 4·8, 6·5, 9·7 and 13·9:1 and the kickstart pedal operated laterally. A friction-damped girder front fork, 8in diameter brakes, tank-top instrument panel with speedometer, crashbars, footshields and large section tyres were standard specification features. The overall engine width was only 20in, saddle height 23in, and despite the low centre of gravity there was 5½in of ground clearance. Price, including full electric lighting and horn, was £72 10s. Though its life was short, the Endeavour is still remembered as one of the best-looking motorcycles ever built.

EXCELSIOR, 1935   Great Britain

AFTER achieving a memorable 1933, 250cc
TT win with a 'surprise' four-radial-valve,
push-rod engined machine, known ever
afterwards as the 'Mechanical Marvel', the
Birmingham Excelsior company was unable
to gain any further success with it. Modifications made in 1934 produced no improve-
ment, and at the end of the season this costly-
to-make model was abandoned in favour of
an entirely new design, the Manxman, which,
although it never won a TT, was twice
second, twice third and during its 1935-58
Island run of appearances earned its riders
numerous replicas.

The Manxman engine was, in fact, one of
the most reliable speed units ever built. It
had an exceptionally massive crankshaft
assembly, and the light-alloy con-rod had
an oversized big-end eye, ribbed for extra
strength. The vertical shaft-drive to the
single overhead camshaft was completely
enclosed and—unusual in 1935—the alloy
cylinder head, with a bronze skull, was
bolted to a cast-iron barrel with alloy

finning. Although the exhaust port was offset to the left, the pipe curved to the offside
round the front down tube of the cradle
frame. The carburettor had a considerable
downward inclination and the float chamber
was remotely mounted on rubber—another
anticipation of what was to become general
practice. Lubrication was by a pump built
into the top of the magneto drive case and
the oil tank had a capacity of one gallon—
vegetable-base racing oil was essential for
these motors. Webb TT-type front fork,
7in diameter brakes with ribbed alloy back
plates, and an Albion four-speed gearbox
made up the general specification. Manxman models, in 250, 350 and 500cc forms,
were initially built as production racers but
roadster types were popular with sporting
clubmen. It is likely that the 1935 350cc
example here pictured began life as a
roadster for, although it is without lights, it
has a kickstarter which was not fitted on the
close-ratio racing gearboxes.

BMW, 1936   Germany

PRESSED-STEEL frames were first used by Bayerische Motoren Werke in 1929 and the beautifully-restored example pictured here, always a centre of admiration when it appears at vintage motorcycle events, is one of a very rare type of which only twenty were imported to Britain, in 1936. The frame, hydraulically-damped fork and the four-speed gearbox are those of the 1935/38 R12 750cc side-valve model but the engine is similar to that of the 1933/34 R16 Series V ohv 750cc machine. Designated the R17, it was produced from 1935 to 1937 and was the last in the pressed-steel series. The mount illustrated, probably for 'export only' reasons, does not have the more elaborate mud-guarding of the German home-market models. Still game for 90mph, the engine has Bosch electrical equipment and direct-to-cylinder Amal-Fischer carburettors. Ridden by Ernst Henne, BMW valve-in-head machines raised the world's solo motor-cycle speed record in three consecutive years, —1935, 1936 and 1937—to 160, 170 and 174 mph.

TRIUMPH, 1938   Great Britain

AUGUST 1937 is a red-letter date in motor-cycling history. It brought the announce-ment of the coming season's red-enamelled Triumph Speed Twin—in the opinion of many the most successful motorcycle ever constructed. Not only has its basic engine layout been continued by its makers, un-interrupted, to the present day, but it has been copied universally. Designer Edward Turner's arrangement of two vertical cylinders paired across the frame was not new. There had been parallel twins many years previously, eg, the Scott two-stroke, and the French Peugeot concern had raced ohc types in the mid-1920s. But the ohv 500cc Speed Twin, or 5T model as it was catalogued, had an engine that embodied the latest design techniques so neatly that, on the engineers' dictum, 'to be right, it must look right', it could not fail to succeed.

In Turner's design the pistons rose and descended side by side, there being a single, central flywheel in the small, robust, barrel-shaped crankcase. Con-rods with split big-ends and shell bearings were used. Transverse camshafts fore and aft of the block operated pushrods in tubes extending up between the cylinders to fully-enclosing, positively-lubricated rocker boxes having screw caps to allow access to the tappet adjusters. A rearward extension of the timing case contained the drive to the Magdyno, above which was the Amal carburettor, feeding through a Y-shaped manifold. Cylinder dimensions were 63mm × 80mm, giving 498cc, and, on a 7 : 1 compression ratio, 26bhp was developed at 6,000rpm, maximum speed being close on 90mph. An oil-bath primary chaincase took the drive to a foot-operated Triumph gearbox whose ratios were 5, 6, 8·65 and 12 : 1. A single front-down-tube, cradle frame, a friction-damped girder fork and a well-proportioned $3\frac{1}{2}$gal tank combined to make up a machine that sold, at £75 complete, in many thousands, saw itself reproduced in many variations, but was not radically changed until 1959 when it became the unit-construction 5TA with over-square dimensions of 69mm × 65·5mm, 489cc—exactly the same measurements as those of the 1973 Daytona 500 model costing over £500.

OVER a period of almost a quarter of a century—from the early 1930s until well into the 1950s—there were no more popular mounts with 'sporting clubman' riders than the Ariel Red Hunters. Designed by Val Page, they originally came in three sizes, 250, 350 and 500cc—all vertical, single-cylinder ohv machines of the two-port type, with Burman four-speed gearboxes, cradle frames and Ariels' own make of girder front fork. They were uncomplicated motorcycles, steered faultlessly, had highly creditable turns of speed and were extremely competitively priced. As a contemporary press tester of the 1938 500cc model depicted wrote; 'Considering the splendid all-round performance combined with good looks and generous equipment, it is rather staggering that the Ariel people at Selly Oak can turn out such machines for £70 10s.' And that included electric lights and horn.

Naturally, during such a long run of production, updating changes occured. The first-off method of carrying the ohv gear on steel plates was altered around 1937 to separate rocker boxes cast integrally with the head (as shown); single-port versions were introduced; and, before the Red Hunters became, in 1954, simply Hunters, telescopic forks and spring frames had been adopted. However, the general specification of the mount illustrated is typical of the 500cc H models at the height of their popularity: 497cc (86·4mm × 85mm); polished ports; high-lift cams; 7·5:1 compression ratio; dry-sump lubrication; large bore, down-draught Amal carburettor; Lucas racing magneto, or Magdyno; gear ratios of 4·7, 6·0, 8·0 and 12·6:1; 7in diameter brakes; scarlet-panelled 3¼gal tank with instrument panel.

Maximum speed could be in the 90mph band but it was mainly in the reliability trials sphere that these mounts showed their competitive worth, carrying many of Britain's expert riders to successes in every kind of endurance event from the club 'mudplug' to Trophy Team honours in International Six Days Trials.

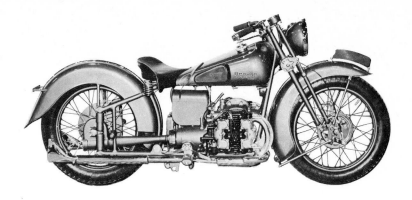

ALTHOUGH his bread-and-butter machines—if the world's then most costly motorcycles could be so called—were all proprietary-engined sv and ohv V-twins, George Brough devised several four-cylinder types during his 1921–39 period as a manufacturer. These included in-line air- and water-cooled units and a transverse air-cooled V-formation layout. None of them was ever quantity-produced and GB's ultimate 'dream' machine, intended as the *ne plus ultra* in motorcycles, could be numbered among the host of aborted 'mounts that never were' which scatter the pages of motorcycling history. When it appeared at the 1938 Earls Court Show, in glistening gilt enamel, it was immediately named the Golden Dream—and so it has remained for, before production could begin, the Nottingham factory was geared to making munitions.

The prototype that took the Show by storm was the joint work of Brough and Freddie Dixon and was an air-cooled, flat-four with one pair of cylinders sited above the other. Single-throw crankshafts were directly geared at the rear of the engine and all four pistons moved inwards and outwards together. On each crankpin one of the big-ends was forked around the other

so that there was no staggering of the cylinders. Drive was taken from the lower shaft through a car-type clutch and four-speed, foot-operated, unit construction gearbox via an enclosed propeller shaft to a worm and wheel assembly on the plunger-sprung rear axle. The Magdyno was flexibly coupled to the top crankshaft, which also drove, by 2:1 chain reduction, a gear-type oil pump in the sump. Alongside the lower sprocket was another which chain-drove the two camshafts running crosswise between the upper and lower cylinder blocks. The all-enclosed overhead valves were push-rod operated.

Cylinder dimensions were 71mm × 63mm, 996cc; each head was a separate casting and the compression ratio was $6\frac{1}{2}$:1. A hand-starting lever mechanism incorporated an anti-backfire device. Gear ratios were 4·2, 6·3, 8·4 and 12·6:1, but a three-speed version with a kickstarter was planned. With a $4\frac{1}{2}$gal tank embodying a rain-drainer, 8in diameter headlamp and 120mph speedometer, the four-speed model illustrated was priced at £185—a dream many would have liked to translate into reality. But Brough Superior production ended with the onset of World War II.

EARLY in 1946 the Birmingham Small Arms Co, to whom Associated Motor Cycles had sold the Sunbeam trade name during World War II, announced an entirely new twin-cylinder machine, designed by Ealing Poppe and named the Sunbeam S7. The picture shows an early prototype machine (the first-off model had a rigid frame). Quantity production did not begin until 1950 when the machine had a car-type cylinder head and chest containing the overhead camshaft valve gear. The carburettor was then mounted on the right between two exhaust manifolds. Thereafter few changes were made to the basic specification which represented at the time one of the most technically-advanced machines produced in Great Britain.

The arrangement of the vertical twin cylinders, crankshaft, clutch and gearbox unit all in line with shaft-drive presented a neat and business-like appearance. Low-pressure 4·50 × 16in tyres provided a super-comfort ride that was further aided by an oil-damped telescopic front fork and plunger rear springing. The chain-driven overhead camshaft carried the coil ignition distributor at its rear end and the pancake dynamo, mounted on the front of the sump, was directly driven from the crankshaft. Cylinder capacity was 487cc, 70mm × 63·5mm, and alternative 6·8 or 7·2 compression ratios were offered. Gear ratios were 5·3, 6·5, 9 and 14·5:1 and the weight was 430lb. A lighter version, the S8, with smaller section tyres and non-interchangeable wheels was also marketed. The original prices were: S7, £259; S8, £227. These machines at first sold readily —by March 1951 10,000 S7 models had been made. But practically no up-dating was undertaken and by 1958, when the types were withdrawn, they had become too costly for the performance they could provide.

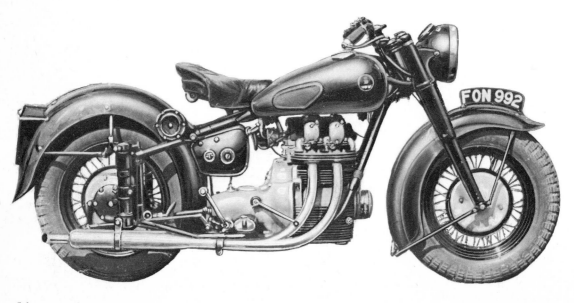

INDIAN, 1948   U.S.A.

FROM their wigwam at Springfield, Mass, the Indian company were still sending forth V-twin 1,000cc Big Chiefs after World War II was over. But when the lighter, livelier British machines, particularly the parallel-twin-cylinder mounts as pioneered by the Triumph Speed Twin, built up popularity with American riders during the late 1940s, an attempt to fight back was made by the Redskins. Their answer to the challenge was based mainly on the Warrior models, which came in 400, 440, 500cc sizes. The picture shows the 1948 440cc (64mm × 76mm) type which developed 28·5bhp at 7,000rpm on a 7·4:1 compression ratio.

With a telescopic front fork and plunger rear springing, the cradle frame was of orthodox English style, but the vertical twin layout was unusual in having both the primary and secondary chain drives on the right. The camshafts, ahead and astern of the cylinder block, operated pushrods in individual tubes leading to four separate, well-finned rocker-boxes. An Amal carburettor was used, ignition was by Auto-Lite battery and coil system with a dynamo mounted above the Indian gearbox whose ratios were 5·38, 6·51, 10·30 and 14·98:1. The gearchange pedal was on the leftside. Dry-sump lubrication, a 4-gal fuel tank and 8in diameter brakes made up the general specification.

In production until 1952, Warriors were the last of the all-American red Indians. When the British Brockhouse company acquired the Indian Sales Corporation a 250cc side-valve Brave model was built at Southport, Lancs, and certain English machines, such as Royal Enfields, were exported to the States with the Indian name on the tanksides. Finally, just before they themselves closed down, AMC Ltd, of Woolwich, bought what was left of a once proudly successful American marque.

EARLY in 1948 the BSA company received an overseas contract to build some 'special purpose' engines and their technicians used a German design, which had come to them as 'spoils of war', as the basis of the units made to fulfil the order. A few months later, they housed one of these motors in a frame of their own design—and one of Britain's most popular lightweights was born.

First called the model D1, it was soon after named the BSA Bantam. In a rigid loop frame, with a light telescopic fork, the engine-unit had a cast-iron barrel, alloy-headed cylinder of 52mm × 58mm, 123cc, bolted to an egg-shaped shell containing the crank assembly, primary transmission and three-speed gear with foot change and kick-starter. Ratios were 7, 11·7 and 22:1, and the power output was 4·5bhp at 5,000 rpm. A flywheel magneto with a direct light-

ing coil was used and with this specification, weighing 155lb and costing £80, the Bantam was an immediate success. In 1949 a plunger-type rear-spring model was introduced and the flywheel magneto was replaced by a Lucas AC generator/battery and coil system. As pictured, the Bantam then cost £95 4s 1d. Maximum speed was 49mph and at a 30mph cruising gait 170 miles could be covered on a gallon of 'petroil' mixture. For 1953 a 148cc D3 Bantam Major joined the range, having, like the smaller machine, a Competition counterpart. It was dropped in 1957 on the introduction of the Super D7 model of 174cc (61·5mm × 58mm) with a pivot-sprung frame. Production of these much-loved two-strokes ceased in the late 1960s but the highly-specialised cult of Bantam racing still flourishes.

VINCENT-HRD, 1949   Great Britain

JUST before Christmas 1955, the last of the big-twin Vincent machines left its factory at Stevenage, Herts. Yet models over twenty years old are still competitive in speed events. The Vincent-HRD story began in 1928 when Philip C. Vincent, a Cambridge undergraduate, left the university to take over Howard R. Davies's Wolverhampton-based HRD marque and to put into practice his own ideas about rear suspension. Production was moved to Stevenage. After a series of proprietary-engined machines had formed the range, a high-camshaft, ohv, single-cylinder type was manufactured and, in 1937, Vincent and Australian designer Phil Irving introduced the Series A 998cc ohv V-twin. This was completely redesigned in 1946 as the Series B, a very much tidied-up machine in which the engine-gear unit formed the major part of the 'frame', the steering head and rear-fork pivot assembly

being bolted to it.

The 1949 Rapide here pictured may be unique in that it is the last machine to carry the Vincent-HRD tank transfer, which makes it a Series B model. But it has the light-alloy-bladed Girdraulic front fork which was introduced for 1950 when the HRD initials were dropped. All subsequent Rapides, Black Shadows, Lightnings, Knights and Princes bore only the name 'Vincent'. All these machines had 998cc (84mm × 90mm) engines, four speeds, dual carburettors, and two brakes on each axle. The price of the Rapide with Girdraulic forks, in 1949, was £323 17s. It weighed approximately 460lb, could top 110mph and had a consumption figure around 65mpg. Just before production ceased, Vincents had captured the world's solo and sidecar all-out speed records.

MAKING their debut at a TT race, the 1951 125cc Lightweight event, the Italian FB-Mondial company entered four machines—and they finished in 1-2-3-4 formation. At the heart of this extraordinary demonstration of speed-reliability was a beautifully-made 123cc dohc engine-gear-unit with deep finning extending around the tunnel for the gear-train cam drive and so deeply and widely cast on the cylinder head that cut-aways had to be made to allow the coiled ends of the hairpin valve springs to protrude into the air stream. In addition to housing the crank assembly and the five-speed gear-cluster, the 'bottom half' encompassed the Marelli magneto.

Although so far in advance in design that it remained a race-winner for many years, the Mondial's power unit was carried in a frame so spindly and simple that it looked old-fashioned when compared with its contemporaries. Eagerness to achieve the highest possible power-to-weight ratio meant that the suspension was almost cruelly rudimentary. Neither the blade-type front fork nor the plunger rear spring units had any sort of damping, and very little movement. Rider comfort was not helped by narrow-section tyres on large-diameter wheels. Results came largely from the little engine's readiness to run up to a then almost unbelievable 12,000rpm, and from the rider's ability to streamline himself on a mattress combination of conventional saddle and padding, hanging his feet on pegs in the rear-spindle region.

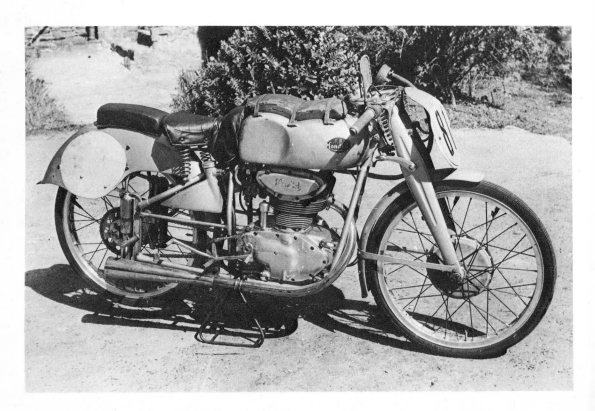

IT WAS in 1946 that the Italian engineering company, Meccanica Verghera, of Cascino Costa, Gallarate, guided by its chief, Count Agusta, turned to motorcycle manufacture—with a simple but well-made 48cc two-stroke runabout. This was followed by a wider range of models, two-strokes and four-strokes, ohv and ohc, as well as scooters. The Count was interested in racing and he engaged an outstanding designer, Ing. P. Remor, to produce a 500cc World Championship contender. Since 1928 Remor had specialized in four-cylinder layouts. He had already designed the Gilera 'four' which was itself based on his Rondine racers. In so far as it used a transverse, air-cooled, double ohc, inclined engine, the resultant MV had much the same essentials as the Gilera, but the in-line shafts of the five-speed gear unit were at right-angles to the crankshaft, this arrangement being necessary to incorporate shaft-drive. Thus, the transmission line turned through two right-angles.

The first models, built in 1950, had torsion-bar springing fore and aft, the front fork being of the blade girder type and the parallel-ruler system of swinging rear fork was friction damped. As with the Gilera, the camshaft drive was by a gear train located between the left and right pairs of cylinders. Two carburettors, each feeding through forked manifolds, were used and the magneto was mounted above the gearbox and gear-driven from the cam train. The duplex cradle frame had an extremely robust fork pivot assembly.

The handling of this machine was not good, and when it was first raced in the Isle of Man (as pictured) by Les Graham it had a telescopic front fork and air-oil control units had replaced the rear friction dampers originally used. Four carburettors now fed the 53mm × 56mm, 492cc engine. A year later the transmission and rear-end were completely re-designed to incorporate a more conventional swinging fork and chain drive. At one period the Earles leading link front fork was used. With ever-increasing speeds, four and three-cylinder MV machines in 350 and 500cc forms have been almost invincible in road racing and at around £2,000 the GT four is the world's most costly 'touring' motorcycle.

SPANISH riders had often competed in international motorcycle events before World War II, but their country had never built any machines that they could use. It was not until 1945 that Francisco X. Bulto, a director of the Barcelona engineering firm of Permanyer SA, formed Motocicletas Montesa, and three years later Montesa motorcycles began seriously to contest the 125cc lightweight class in Europe's grands prix. Senor Bulto's nephew, J. S. Bulto, won his class on one of his uncle's racing two-strokes in the Barcelona GP of 1949. For 1951 the company sent a team to take part in the first 125cc IoM Lightweight TT, and J. S. Bulto and J. M. Llobet finished fifth and sixth, both at speeds well over 60mph. Though unable to match the Italian ohc Mondials on all-out speed, these Spanish miniatures, weighing only 136lb, scored on excellent handling qualities and an ability to hold their maximum gait without stress.

A simple plunger-sprung frame with hydraulic front fork carried a 125cc (54mm × 54mm) engine of unusual design. It had a ported piston, a heavily masked mouth to the crankcase with four fang-like deflectors protruding up into the piston at stroke bottom, and there was an involved set of cylinder ports. In addition to normal 'petroil' lubrication, there was an auxiliary feed to an oil jet in the carburettor intake. The exhaust pipe did not, as it appears to do in the picture of one of the 1951 IoM models, fit into the back of the cylinder but into a right hand side manifold. The horizontally-barrelled carburettor was located opposite on the left side. The impetus which Montesa gave to Spanish influence in the motor-cycle world was boosted when, in 1951, the Derbi and Ossa concerns were formed, also in Barcelona, and in 1958 that city's motorcycle output was further increased when Francisco Bulto founded his own Bultaco company. Today, these four marques share a high proportion of the prizes in international motorcycle sport and provide a considerable part of Europe's answer to Japan's invasion of the world's lightweight market.

NSU, 1953   Germany

FROM 1907 to 1914 and from 1931 to 1939
Germany's pioneer NSU company had been
consistent supporters of the TT races with
350 and 500cc machines. In 1953 they
returned to the Island with two machines,
a single-cylinder 125 and a parallel-twin 250.
Each finished in second place. The 250cc
machine pictured had a pressed-steel backbone type of frame with bottom link front,
and swinging rear, forks, an arrangement
practically the same as the firm's standard
road-going Max mounts. However, the
55·9mm × 50·9mm, 226cc, engine was closely
reminiscent of the pre-war 350 and 500cc
race types, in that it had double-overhead

camshafts operated by two separate, right
side widely-inclined shaft-and-bevel drives.
Although not one of the prettiest motorcycles,
the Rennmax certainly had speed and
stamina, and ended the 1953 season at the
top of the 250cc World's Championship
table. For the following year the whole
machine was completely re-designed, with
a single, leftside shaft driving the dohc
gear. Shorter and narrower than its pre-
decessor, and developing 32bhp, the unit
gave NSU riders the first three places in the
$\frac{1}{4}$-litre Championship and again topped the
league in 1955.

WHEN international motorcycle road racing was interrupted by World War II, super-charged multi-cylinder foreign machines were taking over from the British unblown singles. To counteract this, both Norton and AJS designers had made their plans but in the event, it was only AJS that came up with a tangible answer—a 500cc double-overhead-camshaft, parallel-twin which, because of its 'spiky' cylinder-head finning, was nick-named the 'Porcupine'.

The machine had been planned for super-charging, but post-war racing rules forbade blowers and when the first 'Porcs' appeared in 1947 they were naturally aspirated. The engine-gearbox unit had almost horizontal cylinders with a Y-form gear-train drive to the widely splayed camshafts. Being spur-geared directly to the four-speed box, the engine ran 'backwards.' The crankshaft had

plain journals for the big-ends and central main bearing. A full duplex cradle frame was used with a pivot-type rear fork con-trolled by air-oil spring units. The front fork was of the Teledraulic pattern developed during the war for military machines. Porcupines were consistently raced for eight seasons, being many times modified. But, although successful in grands prix abroad, victory in the Senior TT eluded them, some-times by a 'whisker,' as when in 1949 Les Graham's virtually-certain win was lost through a magneto armature shaft shearing barely a mile from the finish. In 1951 Bill Doran was second and in 1953 Rod Coleman was fourth, on the machine pictured. In its final year of racing the 1954 Porcupine, much altered and with cylinders at 45°, was developing 54bhp at 7,500rpm.

ITALY's famous designer, Ing. P. Remor, who had earlier developed the OPRA and Rondine four-cylinder engines, produced racing machines at Gilera's long-established Arcore factory before World War II and his transverse, water-cooled, supercharged motors not only won international races but broke world records. Post-war, he re-designed the double overhead camshaft engine as an air-cooled, unblown unit, at first using two carburettors, and later four. The camshaft gear train and the geared primary drive were located between the inner cylinders and the transmission chain was on the right of the five-speed integral gearbox. The first Gilera fours had duplex-loop cradle-frames with blade-type girder front and torsion-bar pivoting rear forks and, because of a large, finned oil sump, the inclined-cylinder engine was rather top heavy.

Handling, as well as reliability, was much improved by design changes made for the 1954 season: as can be seen in the picture of Geoff Duke's North-West 200 race machine, a narrow, forwardly-extended sump allowed a lower engine mounting. The two outer carburettors were in-swept to give the rider more knee room and the exhaust pipes were tucked in more closely. Both brakes were of the two-leading shoe type, the rear one having been moved away from the sprocket to the leftside. With a greater power output the engine, 52mm × 58mm, 492cc, pulled a higher gear at slightly lower revs—10,500 instead of 11,000rpm. Suspension had been changed to telescopic front and oil-controlled rear units. By 1957, the 500 model had a 350cc counterpart. They were developing 70 and 52bhp respectively and had a new, short steering-head frame. On these models Bob McIntyre won the Senior and Junior Golden Jubilee TT races and broke the 100mph barrier with the Senior model. After a six-year rest, the 1957 models were de-cocooned to make an Island swan-song when they took second place in both the 1963 Senior and Junior races, as well as a third berth in the Senior. Both Senior machines averaged over 100mph, John Hartle, runner-up to Mike Hailwood (MV), returning a race speed of 103·67 mph.

VELOCETTE, 1956   Great Britain

PERHAPS because its arrival happened to coincide with the post-World War II boom in motor scooters, the Model LE Velocette never reached the rate of production for which its manufacturers had planned. Nevertheless, it was made in large numbers from 1949 to the beginning of the present decade, with only minor changes to its original design. Silent, very well weather-proofed, economical and safe to ride, it was a fine example of the 'everyman' type of machine that so many makers have, over the years, striven to popularise. A great favourite with police forces for beat patrol work, it was nicknamed the 'Noddy bike'; the letters LE were, in fact, an abbreviation of the 'Little Engine', which was how its originators first referred to it.

Nurtured by Eugene Goodman, and incorporating ideas of Australian designer P. E. Irving, the LE was brought into being by Velocette's design-development engineer, Charles Udall. A transverse, horizontally-opposed, water-cooled, side-valve unit, incorporating a three-speed gearbox, was built into a pressed-steel frame. One leg of the pivoted rear fork (with adjustable spring units) housed a propeller shaft that drove the rear axle through a bevel box. Telescopic front fork stanchions passed through the wide and deep mudguard. Legshields, footboards and a hand-starting lever were features. The first LEs had 149cc (44mm × 49mm) engines. For the 1951 season the capacity was raised to 192cc by increasing the bores to 50mm. This changed the price from the original £116 16s to £125, but the overall weight remained the same at 245lb. The LE 200's over-square engine not only raised the top speed to 53mph but was more economical, returning 120mpg averages. The general specification, except for small details such as the adoption in 1956 of a two-level dualseat (as illustrated) and smaller wheels in 1957, was unchanged until 1958 when four-speed, foot-operated gearing was introduced and a kickstarter replaced the lever.

ARIEL, 1959   Great Britain

AFTER some sixty years of building four-stroke machines, the Ariel company shook the motorcycling world in 1958 when its celebrated designer, Valentine Page, produced a 250cc parallel-twin two-stroke 'everyman' mount that was called the Leader. The engine-gear unit was suspended at three points (one of which doubled as the pivot for the swinging rear fork) below a pressed-steel, beam-type frame, on top of which was a dummy tank. The actual 2½gal fuel container was a can-shaped receptacle located between the main frame beams. The pressed-steel stanchions of the oil-damped, trailing-link front fork had only a single crown. A deeply-valanced front guard, a tall, wide screen, dashboard, leg-shields, midships side panels, shrouding over the rear wheel and enclosed chain drive provided a high degree of rider protection. A year later a companion model, having virtually the same basic specification but without the shielding, was introduced as the Arrow (illustrated). It was the last true motorcycle to carry the Ariel emblem.

The Leader/Arrow engine had a light-alloy head on separate cast-iron cylinders, 54mm × 54mm, 249cc, mounted on a light-alloy, die-cast crank-cum-gearcase. Lubrication was by 'petroil', carburation by Amal Monobloc and ignition/lighting by a Lucas AC generator and full-wave rectifier. Gear ratios were 5·9, 7·9, 11 and 19:1. Knock-out spindles through the full-width, cast-iron hubs allowed easy wheel detachment and the silencers were also quickly detachable for cleaning a complex system of baffles. Costing £167 and weighing 275lb, the 1959 Arrow (pictured) was good for speeds around 75mph and could average 80mpg. An indication of its ultimate speed capabilities was demonstrated when a converted-to-racing machine finished seventh in the 1960 Lightweight TT, averaging over 80mph against a leaderboard full of Italian and Japanese factory specials. Ariel production continued when the marque moved from its Selly Oak home to the Small Heath, Birmingham, BSA factory in 1962, but Leaders and Arrows were dropped soon afterwards.

DOUBLE overhead camshaft, single-cylinder racing engines were first used by Norton in 1937, when development engineer Joe Craig modified the Arthur Carrol-designed version of the original CS1 unit. Called Manx Nortons, they were two essentially similar machines, the 30M being a 500cc model and the 40M a 350. They were world-beaters in the hands of some of the world's finest riders and, as production racers, they provided victories for an uncountable number of private owners.

In 1950 fresh impetus to their potentialities came with a change from the conventional brazed-up, plunger-sprung frame to an entirely new layout consisting of duplicated continuous lengths of tubing, formed box-fashion, with their ends welded at the steering head. The rear fork was of the pivot type, controlled by hydraulic spring units anchored to a bolted-on sub-frame.

Front suspension was by the oil-damped Roadholder telescopic fork, developed by Norton during the war. Compared with the old 'garden gate' frame, the new arrangement was so light and comfortable that it was quickly named the Featherbed, and

on its first TT appearance in 1950 Geoff Duke won the Senior race and Artie Bell the Junior, opening a success story unmatched by any other type of single-cylinder racing machine.

Manx Featherbed production models, based each year on the pattern of the factory's latest race-ware, were sold 'over the counter' for eleven years, after which, for some two further seasons, a small number were built to special order. Typical of the 'Bracebridge Street bangers' is the 1959 30M model illustrated. The bevel-driven dohc gear topped a light-alloy head and barrel on a narrow, magnesium-alloy crankcase. Bore and stroke dimensions were 86mm × 85·6mm, 499cc, (76mm × 76·7mm, 348cc, for the 40M) and the standard compression ratio for international fuels was 10·07:1 (10·15:1 in the 350). A Lucas rotating-magnet magneto and Amal GP carburettor were used. Transmission embodied a close-ratio, four-speed gearbox (30M; 4·23, 4·65, 5·63, 7·52:1; 40M; 5·12, 5·64, 6·81, 9·11:1); three-plate clutch; primary chain lubricated by oil carried in the frame. The Roadholder fork had clip-on bars and the rear pivot incorporated bronze-bushed bearings. The 19in diameter wheels had alloy rims, guards, hubs and brake shoes, the 8in diameter front brake being of the two-leading shoe type, 1¾in wide. Rear brake was 7in diameter. The 5gal tank was also in light alloy and the seat base and frontal cowl were fabricated in glassfibre. Weight of the bigger machine was 313lb, the 350 being 5lb lighter. At around £500 apiece, these magnificent mounts had a ready sale and when construction ended completely in 1963 their passing was deeply mourned.

GREEVES, 1967 Great Britain

LATTERLY made almost exclusively for motocross and trials work, Greeves motorcycles first appeared as high-quality, light roadsters in 1952, being the brainchildren of O. B. Greeves, a director of the Thundersley, Essex, firm of invalid carriage makers, Invacar Ltd. Bert Greeves, a confirmed motorcycle enthusiast, had unusual views on frame and suspension design and these are clearly exemplified in this picture of a 1967 197cc Villiers-engined 20DC Sports Single model. A basic feature of Greeves design is a steering head-cum-front down-member consisting of channelled aluminium incorporating a steel top-tube. The leading link fork has bonded-rubber 'spring' units with hydraulic dampers inside the legs. The earlier models also employed rubber suspension for the pivoted rear fork, here shown with proprietary spring units. Unconventional in appearance, these well-engineered, meticulously-finished machines have gained a high reputation for precise handling and lively performance.

ANCESTOR of the present-day Norton Commando motorcycles was the 1949 Dominator model, a 497cc vertical-twin-engined mount that was developed through many stages. The early rigid frame became plunger-sprung, then the Featherbed frame was used; the capacity was increased to 600cc and, just before production was moved in 1963 from Birmingham to the Associated Motor Cycles factory at Woolwich, 650cc types were listed. By 1964 a 750cc model, called the Atlas, was introduced. This had an inclined-engine layout with 73mm × 89mm, 745cc dimensions, a design subsequently used by the successors to AMC, Norton-Villiers, as the basis for all their production units.

It was in 1967 that NV marketed this type of engine in an entirely new Norton model, the Commando, abandoning the Featherbed frame for an ingenious arrangement whereby the engine, the separate gearbox and the

pivot-bearing for the swinging fork were all carried in a sub-frame, rubber-mounted within the main cradle frame. Called the Isolastic principle, the method provides a smooth cushioning effect, absorbing vibration and making for a high degree of frame rigidity. The top frame member is a $2\frac{1}{2}$in diameter tube. The first Commandos, produced for the 1968 season, were given the name 'Fastback' and were similar in appearance to the 1970 model illustrated. Variant models with many improvements, including disc-brakes and power increases, have followed and the Interstate machine has a Combat-type engine developing over 65bhp at 6,000 rpm. NV participation in Production Machine and Formula racing was crowned by first and second places in the 1973 Formula 750 TT, at speeds over 105 and 102mph respectively. The winner, the company's racing development engineer, Peter Williams, set the fastest lap at 107·27 mph.

TRIUMPH, 1972　　　　　　　　　　　　　　**Great Britain**

FOR fifteen years the Triumph Bonneville has held a special place in the affections of riders who appreciate a lusty, urgent engine. This 650cc vertical twin grew out of the

Tiger 110 and Thunderbird models, which were themselves bigger versions of Edward Turner's famous 498cc Speed Twin. The Bonneville made its first appearance in 1958 and has been methodically modified and improved in practically every department, one of the most recent and important departures being the introduction of a re-designed oil-carrying frame with a large diameter saddle tube, top-tube spine and duplex front down tubes. Engine dimensions are 71mm × 82mm, 649cc.

The cylinder block is iron and the one-piece head is in light alloy. Overhead valves are operated in the long-established Triumph manner by pushrods from camshafts lying across the front and back of the crankcase. The crankshaft is carried in ball and roller bearings, and the light alloy con rods have plain, shell-type big-ends. Twin Amal Concentric 30mm carburettors are fitted and

on a compression ratio of 9:1 an output of 47bhp at 7,000rpm is claimed. A duplex primary chain drives a four-speed gearbox having ratios of 4·95, 6·15, 8·3 and 12·1:1. Conical hubs incorporate drum brakes, the front 8in diameter unit being of the two-leading shoe type; the 7in diameter rear brake has single-leading shoe operation. In 1972, the model T120R, as shown, was priced at £596.44, the equipment including Lucas 120-watt 12-volt alternator with full wave-rectifier, Zener diode capacitor, battery and coil ignition, 4gal fuel tank, 150mph speedometer, tachometer, flashers, and a duplicated exhaust system with balance pipe. Weight, 410lb. A 750cc Bonneville has since been added to the range.

BSA, 1972 Great Britain

ROLLS ROYCE made a three-cylinder car in their very early days, but although there have been a number of triple-pot two-stroke motorcycles, four-stroke 'threes' were generally ignored by designers until the MV racers arrived in the mid-1960s. In 1968 the BSA/Triumph group launched such a motor and the former company's version, the Rocket Three, and the Coventry factory's Trident immediately became important contributions to development. As Production and Formula racers both types have achieved prodigious successes.

In general engine-gearbox respects, the machines are similar, but whereas the Trident has its engine vertically mounted, the Rocket's unit is slightly inclined forward. Different frames and tank trim further distinguish them. In the modern Superbike class, the engine is of 740cc (67mm × 70mm), with the transverse, 120° throw, one-piece

crankshaft carried on ball, roller and plain white-metal bearings in a dry-sump crankcase with twin pumps and an oil cooler in the scavenge system. The block and cylinder head are one-piece light alloy castings and the overhead valve gear is operated by pushrods from twin fore and aft gear-driven camshafts. Compression ratio is 9·5:1 and carburation is by three Amal Concentric instruments.

Triple HT coils and contact-breakers are used and the electrics include a Lucas 120 watt, 12 volt alternator with full-wave rectifier and Zener diode voltage control. A triplex primary chain drives the Borg and Beck diaphragm-type clutch and the four-speed gearbox, with right-side change and kickstarter, has ratios of 5·3, 6·3, 8·9 and 12·8:1. The final chaindrive is on the left side. The brazed-up cradle frame has duplex front down tubes and the swinging rear fork is controlled by three-position Girling hydraulically damped spring units. The BSA telescopic front fork has two-way damping. Drum brakes are used, that on the front wheel being an 8in diameter two-leading-shoe type; the rear is a 7in diameter single-leading-shoe component. In the 125mph class, the Rocket Three develops 58bhp at 7,500rpm, weighs 466lb and, with equipment that includes a speedometer and tachometer, cost £691 in the 1972 form illustrated.

MOTO GUZZI, 1972   Italy

FROM Mandello del Lario, on the shores of Italy's Lake Como, has, since 1921, come a continuous stream of Moto Guzzi motorcycles. They have come in all sizes and shapes, from egg-cup capacity mopeds and scooters to thunderous eight-cylinder racers. Two-strokes, four-strokes, practically every method of valve operation and every kind of cylinder configuration have been developed by the company's brilliant engineers, for long headed by Ing. Carcano. And famous models such as the horizontally-barrelled Gambalungha (long leg), its smaller brother, the Gambalunghino, and the wide-angle (120°) V-twin have contributed vivid chapters to racing history in the hands of the world's finest riders.

Guzzi participation in the present-day big-machine category takes the form of high-speed roadsters having a transverse V-twin (90°) ohv engine driving, through helical-gear primary reduction, an in-line integral gearbox and thence by shaft to a right-hand bevel-housing on a rear axle carried in a pivoting fork, one leg of which is the prop-shaft enclosing member. The 1972 V7 750 Sport model pictured has cylinders of 82·5mm × 70·2mm, giving 748cc. Its claimed performance is 70bhp at 7,000rpm (7,300 maximum). The five gear ratios are 4·1, 4·8, 5·8, 7·6 and 10·8:1 and maxima on the two uppermost ratios are 128 and 110 mph respectively. Twin 30mm Dell'Orto carburettors are fitted, giving a cruising consumption figure of 46mpg. The electrical system embodies a 300watt alternator and a $\frac{3}{4}$hp starter motor—there being no kick-starter. A double-sided, 220mm diameter four-leading-shoe brake is used in the hydraulically damped front fork and Koni dampers control the rear spring units. Price: £1,350. A somewhat gentler, less-expensively equipped V7 Special model has been superseded by the V7 GT 850, the 848cc engine of which develops 64bhp at 6,500rpm (119mph). Price: £1,115.

NOT UNTIL the late 1960s were Laverda motorcycles much known outside their home country, Italy. When Moto Laverda was founded in 1950, in Bregance, the range consisted of lightweight mounts from 50 to 250cc with the company's own ohv engines. A 200cc ohv vertical-twin was particularly successful. Then came a policy switch to the other end of the capacity scale, with an impressively luxurious 750cc ohc twin model that soon made its mark in long-distance, particularly 24 hour, races, exhibiting a combination of good handling, high speed and dependability. It could well be that this machine played a leading part in establishing the present-day Superbike trend.

In 1972 the Laverda 750 SF pictured was the sports edition of a pair of models that in general had similar specifications. While the SF was rated at 60bhp at 6,900rpm, the 750 GT produced 52bhp at 6,600. Their claimed maximum speeds were 120 and 110 mph respectively. The inclined, parallel-twin cylinder design employs over-square di-

mensions of 80mm × 74mm, 744cc, and the single overhead camshaft is driven by duplex chain from the centre of the crankshaft, the latter being built up and supported on ball bearings. The big ends have caged rollers in steel con-rods with plain, bushed small-ends. The cylinder head is a one-piece alloy casting; compression ratio 9·7:1. Two 30mm Dell'Orto carburettors are used and ignition is by twin HT coils and battery. Primary drive is by triplex chain and the five-speed gearbox has ratios of 4·6, 5·4, 6·3, 8·7 and 12·1:1. There is no kickstarter, the electric starter being of Bosch manufacture, as is the belt-driven dynamo and the lighting equipment. A spine-type frame, with the engine-unit forming a main support, has swinging rear suspension and a telescopic front fork. Laverda's own cable-operated two-leading-shoe brakes are fitted, 9in diameter front, 8in diameter rear. The 1972 SF model shown, with full equipment, scaled 501lb and the price was £995. A 980cc three-cylinder model was introduced in 1973.

BEFORE World War II Japanese motorcycles were regarded by Westerners as something of a joke. They were mostly poor copies of European types; there was even talk of bamboo frames and ball bearings that were really only lead shot. In 1950 the Honda Motor Company, of Tokyo, began producing mopeds, cyclemotors and lightweight machines of such high quality that they quickly made inroads into the world markets and caused a vast jump in the riding population in their own country. Mr S. Honda, the head of the company, realised the publicity value of competitive sport, and in 1959 he sent a team to the Isle of Man to contest the 125cc Lightweight TT. With virtually no experience of grand prix racing, his men, riding dohc twins, finished 6th, 7th, 8th and 11th and only one machine retired. In the following eight years, Honda machines won eighteen TT races and sixteen Manufacturers' World Championship titles.

A wide variety of Hondas have been made, from 50 to 750cc with single to six-cylinder configurations and dedication to overhead camshaft layout. The 1972 CB500-4 four-cylinder model illustrated owes its ancestry to the racing machine on which Mike Hailwood won the 1967 Senior TT, setting a record lap at 108.77mph which has not yet been bettered. Of 498cc (56mm × 50·6mm), the CB500-4 has its in-line-cylinder, air-cooled engine mounted transversely in a duplex cradle frame. Both the block and the head are one-piece light alloy castings and the one-piece crankshaft is carried in plain shell bearings. The single overhead camshaft is chain-driven from the centre of the crankshaft, as also is the integral five-speed gearbox—the ratios being 5·9, 6·7, 8·2, 10·6 and 15·1:1. Lubrication is on the wet-sump principle with an eccentric rotor pump. Four 22mm Kehini carburettors are used and the electrics incorporate a Hitachi 210 watt 12 volt alternator, coil ignition and a starter motor. Claimed output is 48bhp at 9,000rpm. Chain-driven, the rear wheel is carried in a swinging fork with three-position damping units and a 7in diameter two-leading-shoe brake. The front wheel, in a two-way damped telescopic fork, has a $10\frac{1}{2}$in diameter hydraulically-operated disc brake. Weighing 440lb and luxuriously equipped, the CB500-4 is capable of speeds up to 110mph and in 1972 cost £619. At £750 there is the CB750-4, a 736cc version in the 125mph class.

SUZUKI, 1972   Japan

SINCE its foundation at Hamamatsu in 1952, the Japanese Suzuki marque has progressed from making 50cc motor attachments for bicycles to providing the world with some of the finest motorcycles obtainable—all in two-stroke form. In the course of that progress the company has built a number of ingeniously intricate racing machines. Its twin-cylinder types won the 50cc TT race four times, from 1962 to 1965 inclusive, and in 1965 the marque scored a 1-2-3 success in the 125cc Lightweight race. Direct participation in racing was halted after 1968, but in other forms of competitions, notably in moto-cross, grass racing and trials, Suzukis have continued consistently in the forefront.

Pride of the current range, however, is not a sports mount but a de-luxe, high-speed road machine, the Model 750-3. A water-cooled transverse, three-cylinder piston-ported two-stroke, it has dimensions of 70mm × 64mm, 738cc. Producing 67bhp at 6,500rpm, it delivers its power with the smooth torque of a six-cylinder four-stroke. It can reach 110mph in 60 seconds but it can be 'doddled' gently and quietly through thick traffic or haul a heavy load of rider, passenger and equipment effortlessly into head winds and over hills. Water-cooling allows the use of soft plugs and helps almost completely to eliminate mechanical noise. Behind the radiator there is a multi-bladed electric fan to assist cooling at low speeds. The coolant is pump-circulated. Four ball-races support the crankshaft and the con-rods have caged needle-rollers in both big- and small-ends. The sleeved, light-alloy block and the one-piece cylinder head have highly polished exteriors.

Three Mikuni carburettors are fitted and the exhaust system is branched into four silencers. Posiforce oil injection by pump, with throttle control, forms the lubrication system. Helical gear-drive from between the centre and right side cylinders is taken to a wet multi-plate clutch and the all-indirect cross-over gears give ratios of 4·9, 5·9, 7·14 and 14·9:1. Electrical equipment incorporates coil ignition, a 280watt 12volt alternator and a starter motor. There are two brake drums on the front wheel, each of two-leading-shoe type, 8½in diameter. The rear brake is a single-leading-shoe 8in diameter unit. With a duplex tube frame having twin front-down tubes and tank rails and swinging fork, the 750-3 weighs 498lb and with extremely comprehensive equipment cost £766·50 as pictured.

KAWASAKI, 1972 Japan

ONE of Japan's biggest industrial concerns was founded in Kobe in 1878 by Shozo Kawasaki. It grew to make ships, sub-marines, locomotives, and aeroplanes and it was in 1961 that the aircraft division turned to motorcycle manufacture, influenced by the enormous growth of the movement which had been sparked off ten years earlier by the Honda enterprise in Tokyo. Kawasaki concentrated on two-strokes and the first products were 125cc lightweights and 50cc scooters. Engine sizes increased and when, in 1970, a three-cylinder type was entered in road-racing it achieved second place, in its first season, in the 500cc World's Championship.

Based on this prodigious speedster, the street machine illustrated is the 1972 model H2, a 748cc (70mm × 62mm) air-cooled mount, developing 74bhp at 6,800rpm, with bullet-like acceleration up to a near 125mph maximum. The three separate light-alloy inclined cylinders are steel-sleeved and have individual alloy heads. The in-unit engine base includes a five-speed gear assembly, the primary drive being by straight-cut gears from the right side of the crankshaft; the final chain drive is on the left. Lubrication is by a throttle-controlled pressure system; carburation by three Mikuni 30mm instruments, and magneto-capacitor-discharge ignition with a transistorised LT system is used. A 12volt alternator with full wave rectifier feeds the battery which has many electrical components to look after. An 11½in diameter disc front brake is hydraulically applied, the 8in diameter rear drum brake being rod-operated. Built to the highest engineering standards, lavishly equipped and weighing 435lb, the 1972 Kawasaki H2 was priced at £755 as illustrated.

YAMAHA, 1973   Japan

EXTERNALLY this newcomer to the Yamaha range looks very much like any other modern Superbike. But inside the engine there is a unique-to-Yamaha breakaway from the traditional, and until now thought to be the only practicable method of balancing the reciprocating and rotating components of a 360° crank four-stroke. This type of engine, although capable of perfect balance at the top and bottom dead centre positions, has always been subject to vibration through the action of out-of-balance forces that occur around the mid-stroke phases. Yamaha's Omniphase system overcomes this by using a crankshaft-flywheel assembly balanced to only half the weight of the reciprocating components. A secondary flywheel has a similar mass and is arranged to rotate in an opposite direction by chain drive. Thus, at every stage of a full revolution of the crankshaft proper there is an equal and

opposing force acting through the balance shaft. The chain also drives another shaft, bobweighted to cancel out a rocking couple arising from the positioning of the main weights at different levels.

This clever, yet simple, arrangement gives four-cylinder smoothness to a parallel-twin engine of 743cc (80mm × 74mm) having double overhead camshafts. Named the OHC 750 Electric, the new Omniphase Yamaha produces 63bhp at 6,500rpm and the general specification includes twin 30mm Solex Mikuni carburettors, battery and coil ignition, electric starter, 12 volt alternator lighting, multi-plate wet clutch and five gear ratios of 5·28, 6·05, 7·18, 8·58 and 13·59:1. Braking is by twin-hydraulic 11in diameter discs at the front and a drum on the pivoting rear fork. Weight is 520lb and maximum speed is in the 95mph region.

BMW, 1973   Germany

BY 1939 BMW motorcycles were regarded everywhere as being among the world's finest machines, and a supercharged ohc racer had achieved the supreme accolade of

a Senior TT victory. Post-war production was resumed in 1948—with a single-cylinder 250cc model, and twins followed a year later. In 1950 17,000 two-wheelers were built and the marque was again on the upsurge, reaching an output of 25,000 in 1951/2. But, despite increasing racing success, particularly in the sidecar classes, a sales decline began in 1953 and continued until the end of the decade when it appeared likely that the Munich factory would have to close. Reconstruction saved the company, then concentrating mainly on cars, but towards the late 1960s motorcycle production was down to 6,000 units a year. However, a new, all-ohv range—the 500cc R50/5, 600cc R60/5 and 750cc R75/5—was designed and construction was moved to a new assembly plant at Berlin-Spandau. From 1969 to 1971 output of these machines leaped from 4,700 to 20,000 units yearly and today

'Bee Ems', despite four-figure prices, are being bought as fast as they can be made.

The 745cc (82mm × 70·6mm) model illustrated has the overhead valves operated by pushrods from an underslung camshaft and delivers 57bhp at 6,400rpm. Maximum speed is 110mph (93mph on the third of the four gears) and, with twin, constant-vacuum, diaphragm Bing carburettors, has a cruising fuel consumption of 48mpg. A Bosch 12 volt alternator electric system includes a ½hp starter motor. With a 3·5gal fuel tank, the weight is 419lb and the price is £1,196. A 4·5gal tank is an optional extra that gives this handsome, superbly engineered mile-eater an even more impressive appearance.

IN THE course of some seventy-five years there have been eighty-one different makes of American motorcycles. Only one survives, and Milwaukee, Wisconsin, has been the home of Harley-Davidson machines since 1903 when William S. Harley and Arthur Davidson started to build big-capacity mounts with inlet-over-exhaust valves. Singles of between 350 and 500cc and V-twins from 750 to 1,200cc have been the main products, though during the 1920s a 584cc flat-twin sold well. In the same period the ohv singles, known as the Peashooters, were highly successful in competitions, especially on the early dirt-tracks. In 1959 H-D started to make their own scooters and in 1960 the Italian Aermacchi concern was taken over, thus adding a group of single-cylinder models from 90 to 350cc to the range. For

most people, however, Harley-Davidson means the kind of powerful indestructible machine long familiar to cinema-goers as the American speed-cop's trusty steed.

Top of the present-day range of these types is the model FLH 1200, illustrated. The 1,200cc (84·4mm × 101·6mm), air-cooled twin engine has a built-up crankshaft supported on two taper-roller main bearings on the drive side and duplicated plain journals on the timing side. A forked con-rod assembly keeps the iron cylinders in line, caged rollers being used in the big-ends. Light-alloy heads are topped by enclosed oh valves operated by push rods having hydraulic lifters that eliminate the need for tappet adjustment. Compression ratio is 8:1 and a single, Linkert carburettor is fitted with a large air-cleaner. The coil

ignition electrical system includes a Delco-Remy 12 volt alternator, with solid-state rectifier, and a starter motor. Claimed output is around 60bhp at 4,500rpm. A duplex primary chain drives the four-speed gearbox, operated by a left-side heel-and-toe rocking pedal. Ratios are 3·57, 4·39, 6·50 and 10·74:1; the dry, multi-plate clutch is cable-operated by a handlebar lever in the British fashion.

An immensely strong duplex-down-tube frame has swinging-fork rear suspension with three-position damper units, and the hydraulic front fork is of H-D design and make. Both wheels have 10in diameter hydraulic disc brakes and 5·10 × 16in diameter tyres. Although weighing 722lb, and with a wheelbase of 61½in, the big Harleys have excellent handling qualities and tremendous pulling power, being capable of wafting two people, and as much gear as they can carry, at an effortless cruise rate of around 100mph. Equipped as illustrated, the Model FLH1200 costs £1,695.

PUCH, 1973   Austria

AS IT was Gottlieb Daimler who pioneered petrol-engine transport, it is fitting that his name should be associated with a development that promises, after many years of experimentation, to bring about a new era in vehicle propulsion—the epoch of electric power. In Germany, engineers at the giant Daimler-Benz plant have already produced buses that bid fair to overcome the long-standing disadvantages of conventional lead/acid battery power—heavy weight and limited mileage between re-charges. And in neighbouring Austria, Steyr-Daimler-Puch has been experimenting with an electric two-wheeler—the prototype of which was exhibited at the London Motor Cycle Show in 1972. With this machine, called the Electra, the problems of battery weight and short range still exist, but as mopeds are mostly used for short-distance work, averaging 10-15 miles daily, they are 'wide open' to electrification.

The Puch Electra, which looks very much like any other moped, carries two 12volt, 40 amp-hour car batteries in a container slung low between the wheels. A four-pole DC motor, 500 watts at 4,000rpm, is mounted behind and below the seat pillar. Primary drive to a cross-shaft, that also mounts the pedal cranks, is by toothed belt and the final drive is by roller chain. A fan cools the motor and speed control is by the electronic-pulse system. The machine weighs 128lb, has a cruising speed of 25mph and an operating range of thirty miles between charges. Silent, fume-free, clean, cheap to run and needing hardly any maintenance, the Electra, if produced in sufficient quantity, is expected to cost little more than an equivalent petrol-driven moped.

Acknowledgements

MANY people have kindly spared time and gone to considerable trouble to help me gather the illustrations and information for this book. The sources of those pictures that did not come from my own collection are listed below, but I would like especially to thank the following: Lord Montagu and the librarians at the National Motor Museum (a quarter of the photos came from their archives); Mr Harry Louis, who, while editor-in-chief of *Motor Cycle*, gave me the run of his journal's bound volumes; Messrs B. Manley-Powell and G. Pearce, custodians of the RAC motoring library; Messrs Ivor Davies and Arthur Lupton, of the BSA/Triumph group; Mr Phil Heath, the Vintage MCC's librarian; Mr Bert Greeves, who not only provided pictures of his own machines but also put me in touch with Mr Don Hitchcock, of Folkestone, who acquired some of Mr Greeves's vintage collection; Mr Sammy Miller, who spent a day helping me to photograph treasures in his Aladdin's Cave at New Milton; and Mr Bruce Main-Smith, who has allowed me to reproduce some excellent illustrations from his *Book of Superbike Road Tests*.

The pictures of the machines owned by Messrs J. M. Heanes, B. White and D. Gilbert were taken by me at the Vintage MCC's 12th annual Chiltern Run and I hope that these enthusiasts will feel that my camera has done justice to their magnificently maintained models.

And thanks, too, to Mrs Joan Power for her painstaking transcription of my notes and tapes into typescript.

B.H.

SOURCES OF ILLUSTRATIONS

Photos, Science Museum, London: pp 8, 9, 14, 15, 34, 37, 38, 39, 51, 96; Crown Copyright, Science Museum, London: pp 17 (two), 20, 27 (top); Mr D. Hitchcock, Folkestone, Kent: pp 43, 60; National Motor Museum, Beaulieu, Hants: pp 28, 29, 33, 41, 46, 47, 55 (two), 56, 59, 61, 63, 64, 68, 70, 77, 78, 80, 85, 86, 87, 93, 95, 97; Mr J. M. Heanes, Fleet, Hants: p 32; Mr O. B. Greeves, Benfleet, Essex: pp 35, 99; Triumph Eng. Co. Ltd, Meriden, Warwicks: pp 40, 52, 83; *Motor Cycle*, London: pp 42, 45, 49, 50, 53; BMW Concessionaires GB Ltd, Byfleet, Surrey: pp 44, 109; BSA Ltd, Small Heath, Birmingham: pp 48, 74, 88; Mr S. H. Miller, New Milton, Hants: pp 57, 67, 81, 89; Mr B. White, Hemel Hempstead, Herts: p 58; Mr J. P. Griffith, Bitteswell, Rugby: p 62; Vintage MCC Library, Queniborough, Leics: pp 65, 66, 69, 71, 72, 73, 75, 76, 79; Mr D. Gilbert, Sutton Coldfield, Warwicks: p 82; Norton Villiers Europe Ltd, Andover, Hants: p 100; Bruce Main-Smith & Co Ltd, Leatherhead, Surrey: pp 101, 102, 103, 104, 105, 106, 107; F. H. Warr Ltd, King's Road, London, SW6: p 110; Steyr-Daimler-Puch GB Ltd, Nottingham: p 111.